When New Life Begins

Pushing Past the Old and Embracing the New

A K.I.S.H Home, Inc. Publication

When New Life Begins; Pushing Past the Old and Embracing the New
Copyright © January 2013
By K.I.S.H Home Inc.

Published in the United States of America by
ChosenButterflyPublishing LLC

www.cb-publishing.com
Editing by Danene Baskin, Senior Editor:
Saxifrage.editors@gmail.com
Cover design CTS Graphic Designs

All rights reserved under International Copyright Law. Contents and/or cover may not be reproduced, distributed, or transmitted in any form or by any means or stored in a database or retrieval system, without the prior written consent of the publisher and/or author.

ISBN: 978-0-983163756
First Edition Printing
Printed In the United States of America
January 2013

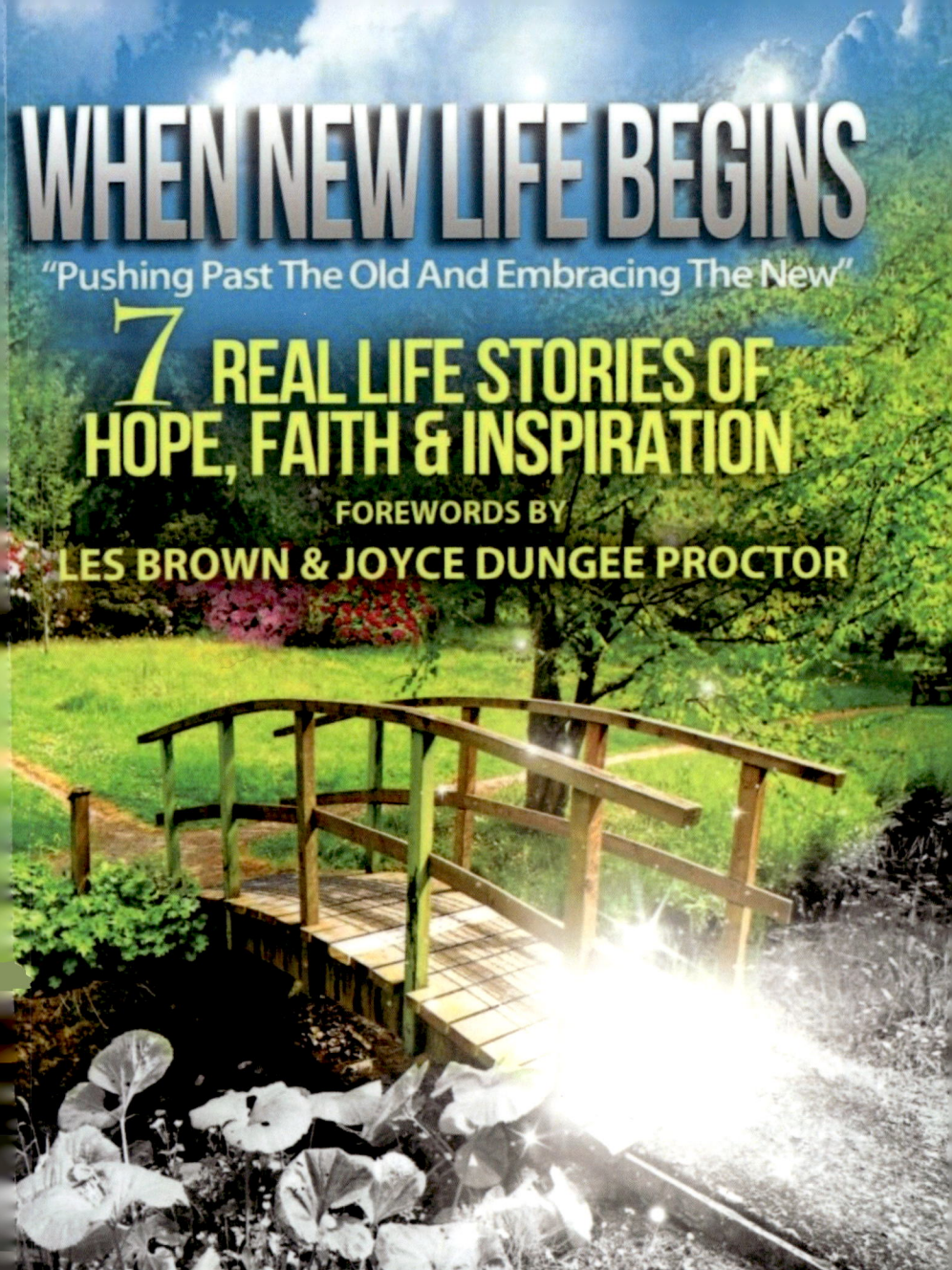

Table of Contents

Foreword by Les Brown................................ v

Foreword by Joyce Dungee Proctor.................vii

Destined to Walk in Victory............................9
    Letisha Galloway

God's Plan... 27
    Natasha Simms

The Dawning of a New Dad........................... 47
    Rodney Davis

The Second Time Around 71
    Ayanna Lynnay

When It All Has To Fall Apart............................ 87
    April Holmes

M.A.L.I.K. 103
    Iyana Davis

True Paradise 119
    Kishma A. George

About K.I.S.H. Home, Inc 141

FOREWORD by Les Brown

Most of the time we think that whatever hardships we are going through as we journey through this world that no one else has it as bad as we do. We tend to feel so alone and helpless in our situation, but reading the collection of "When New Life Begins", you will realize that you are not alone. There is hope. You can have a new beginning by listening to the voice of a higher calling. I'm reminded by a quote by Mother Teresa, "I'm a little pencil in the hand of a writing God, who is sending a love letter to the world," only if you yield to the still small voice provided to us, we have guided instructions to change the world.

There is power in numbers. You can receive great support by reading about seven people with a variety of experiences and challenges in life. Seeing how they overcame their obstacles can give you strength, encouragement, and instruction for your own defeats to come out victoriously on the other side. It is for each one to teach one to see the benefits, the humor, the wisdom, in all things. Remembering to stay humble, in constant faithfulness and gratitude for everything and everyone, while transcending negativity, rising to new and unseen heights.

Between the beautiful, sturdy covers of this magnificent book is an anthology-seven booklets, seven stories, seven lives- the revelations of which will cause spontaneous tears, involuntary goose bumps, and mindboggling astonishment as they edify, and enlighten . "When New Life Begins" is a must-read by all. Once started, it cannot be put down until the last cover is read. You will be uncomfortable after you read this book due to the expansion of your mind and your heart will soon follow.

Rest In Peace to the old You. The old complainer and the old victim. May you begin a new life after experiencing this book. May you be inspired and motivated to seek to have a new beginning in everything! You have Greatness within you and never doubt it!

Les Brown,
Nationally Known Motivational Speaker and Best-Selling Author
www.lesbrown.org

FOREWORD by Joyce Dungee Proctor

What are you supposed to do when life seems unfair? How do you respond when the hand you are dealt is not quite what you desired or anticipated? As you read each descriptive story and situations depicted in this book, you cannot help but ask yourself these questions. The answer is pure and simple, you turn to God.

These inspirational stories will undoubtedly resonate with you in some way. While you might not have experienced the tragic loss of a loved one, or know what it is like to live your life under society's label, you will immediately be able to connect and identify with the resilience, strength and sheer determination exuded in every narration. God wants us to trust Him at all times, no matter what the situation may look like!

Whether it is a negative or bad person, a tragic incident or a situation of apparent despair, that impacts our lives - we must not let the circumstance define who we are, or the path we take. It is most important to learn from the experience itself and rely on God for clarity and direction while maintaining our faith for change, restoration and deliverance for an abundant life.

In reading these stories, I am reminded of Hebrews 11:6, "Without faith it is impossible to please God, because anyone who comes to him must believe that he exists and that he rewards those who earnestly seek him." When you believe, new life begins.

May the Love of God Continue to Bring You Peace Always...

Joyce Dungee Proctor, President
Speaker, Executive Coach, Author and Consultant
www.seminarsbyjoyce.com

When New Life Begins; Pushing Past the Old and Embracing the New

Destined to Walk in Victory

Letisha Galloway

I've always felt that I was destined for greatness. From the time I was a small child I felt something on the inside telling me that I was destined for wondrous things. As a child, the still small voice inside would cause me to try harder, if I didn't succeed the first time. However, as I got older I encountered naysayers and my fair share of blessing-blockers. Throughout my life, it was God who silenced the critics, removed stumbling blocks that I put in my own way and broke every weapon the enemy tried to use against me.

I was born in a small town in New Jersey to a drug-addicted mother and a military father. My parents met in the army. Both had promising careers. My father chose to stay on the right path and my mother made decisions that caused her to become addicted to drugs. I have been asked many times if I believed my father knew about my mother's drug use. My father is a very disciplined individual and I cannot imagine him staying with someone he knew was addicted to drugs and jeopardizing his child. I do not believe my father knew anything about my mother's drug use. Despite being asked by many elders of my family to stop using drugs, my mother continued to use them. The elders warned her of the dangers of doing drugs while pregnant, but she did not listen. Drug addiction is a vicious disease. Addiction caused my mother to care more about getting high than being concerned for her own child that she was carrying.

As with any family, my family was excited about the arrival of a new baby. All of my maternal grandparents and great-grandparents were at the hospital waiting for my arrival. The joy of my arrival soon turned to fear and uncertainty about the quality of life I would have. The very thing that the elders warned my mother about came to pass. I was born with deformities in my legs. I was missing the tibia bone in each leg, and my feet were turned upwards, medically known as clubbed feet. My legs were amputated at approximately 10 months of age. After my amputation, I spent a significant amount of time in the hospital. I am told that I was a fighter even back then.

At the age of 11 months old, I was given to my Great-Grandma Genevieve (everyone called her Genny) to raise, because my mother was still addicted to drugs and my father, as much as he wanted to, could not raise me because he had a career in the military. With the help of my Grandma Genny, I silenced the medical professionals by accomplishing something they said I would never be able to do - I learned how to walk without a cane or walker, using prostheses (artificial limbs).

I learned how to walk unassisted by my great-grandmother taking the time to teach me. She would often put her legs on the outside of mine and guide my steps. When I was younger I always used to tell the story of how my Grandma Genny taught me how to walk on my own. One day my Grandma Genny walked with me from the front porch to the fence in the front yard. She left me by the fence and went back to the porch. I remember her telling me to walk to her. "No", I yelled, and shook my head. She asked me again to walk to her and I finally mustered up enough courage to walk on my own to her. When I arrived on the porch, she gave me the biggest hug and said she loved me.

A lot of my family teased me and said that I could not have possibly remembered that because I was not quite 2 years old. I simply tell them that I *do* remember! Why? I have no idea. Perhaps I remember because it was traumatizing for me at that moment. I remember what I had on that day because it was my favorite outfit that my father bought me.

After I learned to walk on my own, my Grandma Genny made an appointment at a children's hospital in Delaware. When we arrived, my Grandma Genny told me to show the doctors how I can push my baby doll in the stroller. My Grandma Genny told me that I had no problem doing that because I was always taking my doll for a stroll. She then took my stroller away and told me to show the doctors how I can walk. I am told that I was a little hesitant to walk without the stroller but I eventually walked down the hallway to the surprise of the medical professionals who said I could not. The trend of people doubting my ability would continue throughout my life. However, with a praying grandmother and the love of God on the inside, I continued to rise.

Growing up I never knew we were by most standards poor. My Grandma Genny provided for my every need and want. I never knew that our main source of income was her retirement and my disability check. If I wanted a new pair of shoes, new shirt, or the newest CD she went out and got it. She would at times say that she would get me what I wanted later, but she would see the disappointed look on my face and make a way to get it. I often came home to a new outfit at least once a month. I had a happy childhood in the country with my maternal Grandma Genny. We went to the yard sales every Saturday and went on trips to the zoo, parks, and many other places. Some days we would just sit out in the yard and talk. She would tell me that God had a special purpose for my life. She told me that my disability did not change my ability to learn and do well in life because it was only physical.

When I reached school age, there were all types of specialists telling my Grandma Genny that I would be best served in a school for children with developmental disabilities. Thankfully, my grandmother did not listen to anyone, and put me in school with the children from the neighborhood. She gave me a chance. Sometimes in life all we need is for one person to say or show that they believe in us. A kind word or action can spark amazing results in an individual. With the help of that still small voice (God), I continued to persevere, and conquer all obstacles that blocked my blessings.

When New Life Begins; Pushing Past the Old and Embracing the New

In the third grade the teachers decided that I would be best served in remedial classes. They felt that I would feel more comfortable in a smaller class. When I entered public school in the third grade, I was not teased as often as others expected. The children would often ask me if I was in an accident, because I had a limp in my walk. I would tell them that I was born that way, and they accepted it. Occasionally, there would be a new child that transferred to the school and would try to bully me. The bullying did not last long because I would go get a few of my cousins to politely remind them that they should keep their hands to themselves. I come from a very large family. In any given school year, I had no less than 20 cousins in school with me. I was not teased for my physical disability much growing up. I received more teasing for being in remedial classes and my mother being a drug addict.

I excelled quickly in the remedial classes and became very bored after I had completed all of my assignments and often disrupted the class by talking. Eventually a teacher in the eighth grade took the time to tell other educators that I did not belong in all remedial classes. The only academic problem that I had was math. To this day, I am still not an expert when it comes to algebraic equations.

The well-paid educators that were experts in evaluating children disagreed with my 8th grade teacher until my tests showed that I read and spelled well above my grade level. *I am forever indebted to that teacher who believed in my ability to learn.* Unfortunately, some individuals are small-minded enough to group all people with disabilities into one category. Some individuals actually believe that if a person has a physical disability they must have a developmental disability too, and that is inaccurate. A person with a physical disability can perform well academically. A person with a developmental disability can run and complete physical tasks. Disabilities are not interchangeable and are all unique and need to be addressed on an individual case-by case-basis.

For the most part, I had a relatively normal academic and social life. I went on all of the school field trips and tried to walk at the same pace as my classmates. There were times when this attempt was more successful than others. A few field trips required a lot of walking. There were times when I refused to take my wheelchair, because I wanted to fit in. Quite a few times overexerting myself cost me a week in a wheelchair because I had pushed my body too far. When a person wears prosthesis, it is wise to know when to take them off. I often ignored my body's warning me that my skin was breaking down.

One particular time I had just come back from a field trip in Philadelphia and my friends and I had been walking all day. When I got home my legs were so red it looked like I had been sun burned. There were blisters and sores everywhere and I was in excruciating pain. It was painful to even get dressed in the morning. After that particular field trip, I spent a week and a half in a wheelchair because the doctors were afraid that my skin would break down further. It is always dangerous for a skin break down for an amputee because it can cause a need for further amputation. Thankfully, God was watching over me, because I surely pushed my body past its limit.

Throughout school, I was teased by my classmates for having a drug-addicted mother. Often times on a Monday morning I would arrive to people telling me that my mother had been at a local party. It hurt so badly because I thought how could she be at a party less than five minutes away and not come to say hello to me or to check to see if I was still breathing. I didn't understand how a mother could simply abandon her child. I knew my mother was on drugs from the time I was five years old. I did not comprehend at the age of five everything about drugs but I knew they were bad. I waited year after year for my mother to come back and get me. I said to myself each year that this would be the year that she would get clean and come for me.

Throughout my life, I would see my mother once or twice a year. I have been told my entire life that the reason my mother did not come around to see me is that she did not want to see my disability. I was unable to understand how that was my fault. It wasn't my choice to come into this world and I certainly had no choice of whether or not to accept the physical position she put me in by doing drugs while pregnant. I longed for a mother-daughter relationship until age nine.

I will never forget it. My grandmother and I were in the car about to leave for my ninth birthday party and I heard my mother yell for us to wait as she ran towards the car. I was excited to see my mother. My excitement soon turned to disgust because I could smell the alcohol coming out of my mother's pores and she appeared to be high. A nine year old should never know what a high person looks like but I had seen it plenty of times before and I knew she was indeed high. My grandmother told her not to embarrass us at the party. My mother said okay. I was embarrassed because my close friends were at the party and they knew my mother partied and was a drug addict. I did not want them to see her. I refused to be teased anymore about my mother or her drugs. It was on my 9th birthday that I decided my Grandma Genny and father were enough and that my mother would never love me the way a mother should. At the age of nine I let go of the dream of having a relationship with my mother. I fought throughout my life to be the total opposite of my mother. I heard the occasional "you are going to be just like your mother." I so despised that phrase. I was nothing like my mother. I set goals and expectations for myself. At times some people thought my goals were too high.

As I prepared to enter high school, I had many ideas of what I wanted my occupation to be when I graduated. I will never forget the meeting with my guidance counselor that I had in ninth grade. I informed him that I wanted to be either a social worker or a lawyer. The guidance counselor informed me that he did not think I was college material. He said that I should start working towards a trade. I had entered the office full of hope and dreams and left feeling defeated. I thought perhaps the counselor was right; it was his job to guide students. I ignored the voice within (God), and the next school year I enrolled in trade school for half of the school day. I excelled in the nursing assistant program but that was not what I wanted. I desired to go to a college or university and be interactive in a lecture hall setting. I settled on secretarial/business trade program in the eleventh grade. Once again I excelled in the program, even though math was not my strongest subject.

In one year I managed to do what I wanted instead of listening to God and ended up with no solid trade because my last year in high school I switched trades yet again and went into child care. I wasted three full school years listening to man instead of God. If I had taken the time to consult God, I would have known that a trade is not the path I should have taken. Listening to God has the best advantages because He already knows where He wants you to go in life and all we have to do is to be obedient and listen. When we fail to listen we hinder our own progression in life. If we pray and ask for guidance from God and listen, I mean really listen, He will guide us back to the life He designed just for us.

After my Grandma Genny passed in 1998 from cancer, I lost my way. I struggled with my self-esteem because she was the one who always told me that I was beautiful and smart. By this time my great uncle had moved into the home to be my guardian. He always encouraged me to do better and to reach higher. If I brought home a grade of "B" he wanted to know if

I had really studied hard enough. Most of the time, I had not pushed myself as far academically as I could have. His encouragement pushed me past "just good enough" and into excellence. Even though I had my uncle speaking words of encouragement in my life, there were always other people speaking negativity. Instead of listening to my uncle who told me that I could do more in life, I listened to the wave of self-esteem crushers. Now that my grandmother was gone, I had people telling me that I was less, and that what I was doing was not good enough. The way I walked in my prostheses was not good enough, my grades were not good enough, and that I could stand to lose some weight. I never thought that I needed to lose weight. I was not a stick figure but I was not large either.

Back in 1998 I was every bit of 160. While that was not obese, I developed an eating disorder and went down to 120 pounds in a matter of less than two months. I felt good about my new physique and received compliments. *Sometimes making others happy can cost you big time.* A few times during school I nearly passed out because I was not eating. At one point my blood pressure was too low. I always knew about high blood pressure but I never knew it could be too low. I continued to be defiant and not listen to the voice telling me that if I kept listening to others I would pay for it. I continued to drop more and more weight; I had finally reached 108 pounds. Then it happened, I passed out at school. I was more embarrassed than hurt; I had finally decided that I should accept myself the way God made me.

Sometimes it takes God making us fall because we will not listen to bring about a change. Now that I was accepting of my physical appearance, I needed to be confident in my intellect as well. After high school I spent a few years pondering if I was good enough for college. I asked myself every day if I was smart enough. Many people told me that it was too late for me to start college. I was told that I should "get real" and get a job. I entered college in the spring of 2002. I was confident that my college career was the start of something life changing. I would feel confident one semester and do extremely well. After the semester ended I would share my accomplishments with others and most were happy for me, but a select few always had something negative to say about my attending college. Instead of listening to the majority, I listened to the minority. I internalized all of the negative comments and failed three semesters before being finally removed from financial aid.

After the removal from financial aid, I felt defeated and like an all-around failure in life. I stayed home wallowing in self-pity and defeat for months. Finally, a voice on the inside said, "That's enough! Get up!" I did just that. I packed up my belongings and in 30 days I moved to Dover, Delaware. My great-great aunt (who raised my sisters) welcomed me into her already- crowded home. She did not complain even once about me being there, and told me that I could stay as long as I needed to. The day after I arrived in Dover I went over to the local community college and signed up for the spring 2005 semester. When I entered the building, I had not a clue where I was going or who to talk to. I finally reached the admissions desk and completed my application. I was then directed to financial aid. I was a bit apprehensive about financial aid because I was removed from it in New Jersey after 3 very trying semesters. I explained to the financial aid officer that some terrible things had occurred in my life that caused me to lose focus in college. I told her that I was ready to move forward. She informed me that my financial aid should not be an issue and she strongly urged me to make an appointment with Student Support Services the following week. The following week I met with a counselor at Student Support Services who would change my life. The counselor asked me what my goals were and told me how they could help me get there. I told the counselor that I wanted to finish at the community college and then get my Bachelor's degree. He asked me why I wanted to stop at a Bachelor's degree when I was smart enough for a Master's degree. I told him that I never really thought that far into an academic career. The way this counselor spoke I could tell he was a man of faith. After several appointments, I became more and more confident in my abilities. I began to think what I can do after my Master's degree. A word of encouragement can go a long way.

    In the fall of 2007, I transferred to Wilmington University as a Criminal Justice major. I had a made-up mind. I knew this time that I would finish college. I studied harder than I had ever studied before. I took 6 classes per semester. I completed my program ahead of schedule. I finished my program in fall of 2008. I attended graduation in January of 2009. It was one of the proudest moments of my life. My maternal grandmother and step-grandfather made it to the ceremony. Others in attendance included my uncle (mother's brother), my baby sister, and my niece. My mother actually made it to the ceremony, as well. I should mention that while we do not have a relationship, she has been clean over 8 years now, and is a much better person for it. I felt a lot of love that day. I felt the spirit of my maternal great-grandmother with me, and I wanted her to know that all of her sacrifices were not in vain. In the fall of 2009, I started a Master's program at Wilmington University. What the counselor spoke had come to pass. I was on the path to completing a Master's degree.

Moving to Delaware changed my life. I started to attend church on a regular basis. Previously, I was absent from church an entire 2 years. It felt good to get up in the morning and give God the glory. In church there were so many loving people, I forgot what it felt like to be in the house of the Lord. I grew up reading the Bible, singing in the choir, and praying. I had wandered off into the world away from God. Thankfully, the values that my grandmother instilled in me did not let me wander too far for too long. Wandering away from God is like going into the woods without a compass; sure you may make it out, but why chance it?

I have learned to listen to God. If what I want is not in agreement with God, I pray that He take away the desire for me to have it. Today, I am on the path to fulfilling my destiny, because I am being obedient to God. We all fall sometimes, but we must remember that dirt can be washed off. God is in the business of restoring lost souls. He wants to see us happy and give us the desires of our heart. We must accept that man will stumble and disappoint us. Man is not perfect and we should not listen to man to find the path to our God-given destiny. God has given us a destiny, not man; so we must honor him. The way we honor God is by being obedient so He can bless us and the blessings are for the whole world to see and to know that we serve a God of prosperity.

There will always be negative people telling you that something cannot be achieved. It is important to remember that God gave life and the dreams that live inside of us. Man is not the giver of dreams so he does not have the power, alone, to take them away. When we doubt ourselves, we give the dream-snatcher the power to succeed. When we remember to acknowledge God every day and thank Him for the gift of the dream He put into our hearts, we become more powerful and are propelled further into our God given destiny.

Today, I am a Senior Social Worker for the Division of Social Services. I have a Master's degree in Administration of Human Services from Wilmington University. I am currently working on a second Masters in Criminal Behavior. I am confident that my accomplishments do not end here. My goals for the future include: writing books, being a motivational speaker, becoming the director of a program and completing a doctorate degree. I was recently informed that many back in my hometown are surprised that I am doing so well. A child of God doing well in life should never come as a surprise or shock to anyone. My greatest hope is that people realize that they must get out of their own way and learn to trust God. It has taken me a long time to learn that lesson and there are still times that I forget but I am quick to remind myself that God is in control and to just step aside. Wherever God is taking me, I am ready and willing to follow Him, for He knows what is best for me and what path I should walk. Despite all that I have been through, I now realize that I was destined to walk in victory!

Letisha N. Galloway

grew up in Woodstown, New Jersey and currently resides in Delaware. She obtained a Bachelor of Science degree in Criminal Justice from Wilmington University. She obtained a Master of Science degree in Administration of Human Services from Wilmington University. Ms. Galloway is presently a Senior Social Worker/Case Manager in Delaware.

Ms. Galloway is a poet, author and inspirational speaker. Her debut novel Victim to Victor will be available in the summer of 2013. In her debut novel Ms. Galloway will take readers on a journey through her life as a double amputee, domestic violence survivor, and multiple other turning points in her life. Her greatest hope is to inspire others to realize that their past does not determine their worth or their God given destiny.

Ms. Galloway is the mother of one, a son she named Jordan who is resting peacefully in the arms of God. Her activities include but are not limited to being an active member of New Jerusalem Baptist Church under the leadership of her uncle Pastor and Founder C.V. Holmes. Additionally, she is the co chair of her church's scholarship fund. She may be contacted at victimtovictor2013@gmail.com

Letisha's Acknowledgements:

First, I would like to thank God for leading me through this incredible journey. Thank you to K.I.S.H. Home, Inc. for this blessed opportunity. Thank you to my Dad for being supportive and wanting only the best for me. Thank you to my Stepmother, and brother Jay for their support. Thank you to my Grammy Mary, for keeping me in prayer. Thank you to my Uncle Larry who pushed me to reach a little higher in life. To my Aunt Cecelia thanks for your encouragement. Thank you to my sisters Kris and Kym who I can always count on for a smile or a joke to brighten my day. Thank you to my Uncle and Pastor C.V. Holmes for his guidance. Thank you to my friends who have supported me Kim, Shanda, Victoria, Cassie, Lydia, and many others. Thank you to my cousin Natalie who always supported my dreams. Thank you to my cousin Sheri who has given me guidance, love, and support. To my Aunt Freddy I want to say thank you for always being there to listen. Thank you to all of my family that have shown their love. Thank you to the members of New Jerusalem Baptist Church for their love and kindness. Last but not least, I want to thank my two angels in heaven my son Jordan thank you for teaching me what it is to love, and Grandma Genny thanks for all of the life lessons you taught me, and for loving me unconditionally.

When New Life Begins; Pushing Past the Old and Embracing the New

God's Plan..

Natasha Simms

"For I know the plans I have for you", declares the Lord; "plans to prosper you, and not to harm you, plans to give you hope and a future" ~ Jeremiah 29:11

September 13, 2002 was the day that I decided to disregard all of God's plans for my life and execute my own. It was the day that I ultimately began my "40 year" journey through the wilderness. Two weeks leading up to that date, I remember various friends, and even mere acquaintances warning me not to marry Jason, along with co-workers filling me in on the dirt that he was doing with other women; and him quitting his job even though we were getting married in 2 months. I still felt that he was "the one" for me.

I stopped praying and going to church early into the relationship. My relationship with God was no longer existent. I can remember my best friend Lisa telling me that my former pastor who had never met my future husband nor knew that I was getting married, instructed Lisa to tell me that God said Jason was not my husband. Amidst the Godly prophetic warning, it fell on deaf ears.

The walk started roughly as expected. I remember staying at my apartment that night and waking up to observe him leaving for the whole next day. The problems only became bigger. To sum it up, he had gotten another woman pregnant a day before we got married and another one pregnant a week afterwards. Even though these things were happening, I still decided to stick it out in the marriage. Exodus 20:5 reads *"Though shalt not bow down thyself to them, nor serve them: for I am the Lord thy God am a jealous God."* Because I did not remove Jason out of my life willingly; God did it himself!

October 19, 2004, Jason had been out all night making drug deals. I told him the night before that I felt like this would be our last night together. He got up the next morning and left, not paying me any mind when I begged him to stay home with me. Hours later the police were banging on my front door. I let them in. They explained that they had Jason and wanted to know where the drugs were. I quickly told them.

I was arrested and walked out of my apartment 8 months pregnant, handcuffed and with a whole crowd of onlookers whispering. As soon as the police got me processed, I had to go through the embarrassing ordeal of being strip searched. The female officer conducting the search said to me with sympathy in her eyes "such a pretty girl with such a loser." Long story short, Jason ended up telling me that he wanted me to take his drug charge because the judge would not give me any time being that it was my first charge. I agreed to it *(yeah I know, so stupid*). I also paid for his lawyer, while I had a public defender.

Finally, right before the hearing, a light came on and I told Jason that I loved myself and my children way more than him and could not take the charge. Jason plainly said to me that if I didn't do it willingly then we would have to let the court decide whose drugs they were. I questioned myself what kind of man does that? *A man that the Lord did not send to you.* Ultimately I decided to become a witness for the state and testify that the drugs were Jason's, if he did not voluntarily do it himself. Jason saw it my way. They ended up giving him 8 years. I received a year on probation and a felony, on top of losing my children and my apartment. Our marriage was over physically but I did not file for a divorce. I thought out of sight out of mind. I began to become involved with other men although I was still legally married. I was willfully and knowingly operating as an adulteress which was backward thinking!!

Instead of running to God, I ran further away all the way down the wide road Matthew 7:13 talks about. *"Enter ye in at the strait gate: for wide is the gate, and broad is the way, that leadeth to destruction, and many there be which go in thereat."* I began using drugs heavily, drinking constantly, sleeping with multiple men and women. I lost my job due to showing up late frequently, especially on the mornings after heavy pill popping and partying. I lost everything; in and out. I was looking to fill the void and hurt I felt in my heart with substitutions and false happiness that comes with drugs and men.

I was close to my bottom but somehow convinced myself that I was at the top. I began to hang around individuals who stated that they knew God and He was in their hearts, but they carried themselves in a way that was contradictory to those statements. I was guilty of it as well. That is why I felt comfortable around them. We were walking in the fruit of the flesh as Galatians 5:19-20 message *"It is obvious what kind of life develops out of trying to get your own way all the time, repetitive, loveless, cheap sex, a stinking accumulation of mental and garbage; frenzied and joyless grabs for happiness; trinket Gods; magic show religion; paranoid loneliness; cut throat competition; all consuming yet never satisfied wants, a brutal temper; an impotence to love or be loved; divided homes and divided lives; small minded and lopsided pursuits; the vicious habit of depersonalizing everyone into a rival; uncontrolled and uncontrollable addictions; ugly parodies of community."* I operated in all these fruits of the flesh from beginning to end.

It is funny how a person can think that they are having the time of their lives, eating off of these fruits but in reality slowly dying. I was taking small steps toward eternal damnation, but like many people, I did not care. I was having a "good time" doing my own thing. Me following my own path has led to my doing a lot of things that could have gotten me killed or very sick. I mean, I could have lost my mind!

I remember taking these 2 pills that I was warned not to do. I was at a friend's party. I went outside and sat in the car. I woke up the next day in my mother's house in my bed. I do not remember anything of that night at all. What I found out was that I passed out in the car and a friend of mine tried to wake me up. However, I did not, so they drove me home and carried me up the stairs. I could have been raped or killed. Thank God for His mercy!

Proverbs 13:15 says *"good understanding giveth favor: but the way of transgressors is hard."* One would think that a person would learn their lesson. Nope! I only got worse. My children, of custody whom I lost, were living with my mother and mother-in-law. I barely saw them. I was too busy "doing me". I moved to New York for about three months (my own plans). However, I missed my kids and spent all of my money. I had to come home. Countless nights, different names and faces, but to me it was all the same - temporary fixes to a hurt that only an Eternal Father could heal.

I would run into individuals who were looking for a fix as well. I was so quick to tell them about God and how good He was, however, my actions preceded my words and they did as I did. Sometimes I think about all of the opportunities that I had to lead people to Christ, but because I was caught up into my own selfish wants I paid no mind to them. *I thank God for His forgiving power and grace!* There were souls that I was attached to and I used my gifts of talking, charm, and laughter and influence to lead them into the wrong direction, and that did not matter to me. No matter how much I said it did, it really did not.

There were many times that people I did not know or briefly knew would ask me why I was hanging around the people I knew. They would say, "You do not belong out here" or "you do not fit in." I did not like those comments. I *wanted* to fit in. I wanted to belong, no matter what it cost me.

I have been around prostitutes, pimps, drug addicts, drug dealers, gold diggers and party girls, but was never fully satisfied with what those different lives gave me. And although God was everywhere I went, watching me, the enemy was as well, and he made that very apparent a few times. One time I was sitting in the car of my friend who would periodically come to check up on me and witness to me. I was getting ready to go to the club when he came. I got in the car and he began ministering to me. No sooner had he started, than that my cousin who was 14 at the time, came skipping out of the house and began skipping around the car chanting: "You're going to miss it; they are going out and are going to leave you." Tim, my friend in the car, said to me: "You know who that is, right?" I said: "The devil." As soon as I said that, she came up to my window, looked in, and while giving quotation signs with her hand, said: "It's nice knowing you." I didn't even look at her, it was her voice but I heard someone else. I began to cry. It was the enemy. Tim prayed for me; however, I went out anyway.

It is funny how we can be quickly reminded how real God and the enemy is, but become quickly distracted and forget what is really on the line. I remember reading the book *'Divine Revelation of HELL'*, and was scared out of my wits. I could not sleep at night worrying about how real hell was, but just like any other time, that fear lasted temporarily. I had to have my own personal divine experience with God in order to be changed.

Towards the end of my run, I slowed down on going out and changed my friends, and because I had completed all of the drug classes and probation required of me by the courts, I was able to regain custody of my children. God blessed me with another job and a brand new town-home through a transitional housing program in which I could participate for two years and have the chance of going back to school.

In the meantime, I was introduced to a gentleman named David, who seemed to be God-sent, but how could that be? He was married, as was I. This guy gave me the story that he and his wife were still living with each other. However, they were separated, and I chose to believe him. He was charming, good looking, well-spoken and 10 years older than I was. This guy went to church with me, bought me books on how to be a better Christian, encouraged me to find God. I thought I found my husband. I know that sounds crazy, but when we lust after our own fleshly desires we will make what is obviously wrong seem so very right.

Soon after, David and I began doing various drugs together and going to parties. He would stay at my house. I questioned his marriage about 5 months into the "relationship". After a while, I could care less as long as I had him. I got pregnant by David and he convinced me to abort the baby. I was so hurt by that decision. David did not pay for the procedure. He dropped me off, picked me up and never checked on me again. David never looked out for me. Although he gave me money and bought me a car, when I really needed him to be around, he was never there. Why? Because he was someone else's husband. I vowed to stay away from him. However, that did not last. I had an ungodly soul-tie with him as I had had with many other men. I was "in love"; or so I thought; more like in LUST. As expected, I became pregnant again. However I refused to go through an abortion as I had before. David urged me to do it, but I just could not. I was two months pregnant when I made that decision, which ultimately ended our "relationship".

That point in life was the beginning of the turnaround in my life. Although I told him I was not going to get an abortion, I was still contemplating on doing it. I continued to smoke weed, and drink, until one Sunday I decided to go to church. My friend Tina and I decided that we would go to church and then go to a barbeque in the neighborhood. I sat in the church and listened to the preacher as he made the altar call and I found myself going up to the front. He made his way over to me and said something I will never forget, *"Therefore come out from them and be separate, says the Lord. Touch no unclean thing, and I will receive you"* (2 Corinthians 6:17). It was his voice but it felt like it was God speaking directly to me.

That moment changed my life forever. I returned to my seat and felt like a veil had been lifted off of my eyes. Tina and I went to the barbeque as planned. When I was offered to take a puff of the blunt, I quickly said that I did not belong there and left. I called Tim up immediately and asked him to come by my house. I explained everything that happened. Tim came by many days out of the week and prayed with me, read the Bible with me, ministered to me and encouraged me.

As time went by, I stayed in the Word, prayed continuously and fasted. God totally separated me from those around me. This made many people upset. However it was the will of the Lord. God totally took the wanting taste of alcohol, sex, drugs, secular music and foul language out of my mouth.

I remember being in prayer and God saying to me that I had to get rid of all of those things that were attached to my past: my club pictures, my scandalous clothes, my toys, my movies and the television and car David bought me. I did it without question because He told me that is what man does, I can do better! And I believed Him. I totally depend on God for everything.

My friend Tina and I had grown apart at that time, although I loved her like my own sister. God was telling me that it was time to separate myself from her. It was New Year's Eve, and Tina and I had decided to go to church. We were standing next to one another when my bishop directed the crowd to close their eyes and ask the Holy Spirit to reveal to them whom they needed to remove out of their lives. Instantly her face popped up. I was not trying to see that, so I held on a little while longer. While I was going higher in God, Tina was still doing the same things I once partook of with her.

A month later, I received another message from God through my next door neighbor that He wanted me to separate myself from her immediately. So I did. No sooner after I did that, Tina literally lost her mind. She called me one day and stated that she had bad spirits in her house and that she was scared to stay in there. I later found out that she had checked herself and her children into a hotel because of their fear. Tina was walking around with bandages on her head and patches on her eyes telling people that the spirits in her house beat her up. This was the reason God had me separate myself from her. If I had not allowed God to come into my life and been obedient to His warning, I could have ended up just like her.

When I look back over my life and see all of the situations I was in, I realize God has truly been keeping me, even when I did not want to be kept. That is what God will do; keep us, love us and care for us even when we do not do it for ourselves. So many of the people I have hung around, dealt with or talked to, have died, lost their minds, been locked up or are still walking around looking to fill their void. I am so glad God rescued me when He did.

I had joined a local church. This was exactly what I needed-- fellowship with other believers -- those who had been where I was and could help me with my walk. The enemy will try to convince us that we can handle everything by ourselves; that we do not need any help; but that is not the case. We need help and should not be ashamed to ask for it.

I thank God for the church that He placed me in. They have been so instrumental in my life. All through this time, I was still pregnant with David's baby boy. I made a vow to God that I would not have sex until I was married again, especially after He spared me from a life of HIV. The enemy had me convinced that I contracted it. When I got my first initial test and second tests done, they both showed up negative. I knew that my body belonged to God, because I really should have contracted that disease.

I totally left men alone and made God my companion as He should have been in the first place. I went through my pregnancy alone, which at times hurt me. However, God gave me a "midwife", Aunt Blue, who was always there spiritually, physically and emotionally. She was my best friend's mother and was always there cooking and cleaning for me, staying over at my house and making sure I made it to doctors' appointments. I appreciated God placing her in my life at that time. He knew what and whom I needed at the exact time and supplied it. *"But my God shall supply all your need according to his riches in glory by Christ Jesus"* (Philippians 4:19).

My landlord, who was the director of the transitional program, gave me a job at the shelter adjacent to my house. I began working at the shelter, taking my Word (Bible) with me. God worked through me so much in that place and it was so evident to those who needed Him the most. It was not "my plan" to go over to the shelter and pray for people, but that is what God called for.

Believe you me; I was not comfortable with praying for folks out loud. If they asked me to pray for them, I would do it. When I got home, however, more and more frequently individuals would ask me to pray for them right at that moment, so I had to put away all of my own thoughts and do what they asked. Working at that shelter blessed me so much. When I sit back and think about all the lives God touched through me, I smile. I mean being in a place where people are "at their worst" and are most vulnerable to the enemy, God puts me in a place that allows me to minister to them, even if it is just with a simple smile.

This helped me to grow so much. I realized that God will meet us right where we are, but we have to be open to receive Him. If I would have been caught up with my own issues, I would not have been effective. Not only was I working, I was able to go back to college. The time came for me to have my baby. When I look at him, I realize, every day, that if I had gone by my own plans, he would not have been here. But because God intervened on his behalf, my son is here.

This walk has not always been smiles and laughs, but because of God, even on my bad days, I still had hope and knew that these times were only to make me stronger. *"Trust in the LORD with all your heart and lean not on your own understanding"* (Proverbs 3:5). That's why going to the Word is so important because without it, we would not have clues as to the nature of God.

I finally divorced Jason in 2009. I met and talked to some nice gentlemen. However, they were not in God's plan for me and He would make it so obviously clear to me. A lot of times I would get down because of the lack of physical companionship. I remember one instance where I was talking to this guy named John. He was a nice guy. We had been talking and hanging out. Finally, I felt the need to tell him about the vow that I had taken. Immediately John sounded disappointed, saying to me, "What guy messed this up? You will never meet anyone who will be willing to wait until then!" I explained to him my stand. He stated that he knew that I was too good to be true, and that he could no longer be my friend. Talk about hurt! I laid in my bed that night and cried my eyes out asking God why.

The next night I was sitting in my room watching TBN and reading a book by a prominent Christian leader. I got to the chapter where the title was Jeremiah 1:5 *"Before I formed you in the womb I knew you, before you were born I set you apart; I appointed you as a prophet to the nations."* I kind of paid it no mind. I was still hurting from the events that transpired the night before. While watching TV, there was a preacher there. As he stood up, he began to say, "This message is especially to the person sitting on the bed crying asking God why? Did I make the wrong decision?" God said ... and he quoted Jeremiah 1:5. My mouth dropped to the bed! I felt like he was talking to me. I could not believe it! I began to cry and looked down to another page in the book and saw the scripture again. It popped out, and I could not see anything else. At that moment God met me in my bedroom and encouraged me. I felt like my father had been sitting in there with me listening to me cry, and in an instant took His tissue (Word) and dried up all of my tears. Yeah, it is hard at times, but I know that my Father knows best. He promised me that I would not have to go through what I went through before.

My two years were up in the transitional program that required me to move into another residence. This time it was not through a program. I had one more year left in, and my job at the shelter had to end because of the agency closing down. For two years I was out of work; however, my children and I never wanted for anything. I had a car, my own apartment, bills paid, food, and we had clothes on our back. God began to make very clear His plans for my life.

I went to a revival service at my church. A visiting pastor came and called me up to the front. This prophet of God revealed God's plan for me. A year later, the same prophet came back and repeated the same exact thing to me. The prophet returned the following year. Do you know that this man of God prophesied the same exact thing to me as he did the two previous years before? However, he stated, "*The steps of a good man are ordered by the LORD.*"

How much does God love me that He would allow His prophet, a man who does not personally know me, or could have possibly remembered me, repeat the same prophecy to me 3 years in a row. It was God establishing His Word to me concerning my life. That's how great the God that we serve is. He never leaves us in the dark concerning our lives. It is we that must stay close to His ear and make sure we are obedient to His Word.

I had applied for a pardon from the governor in May of 2011; however, a close friend of mine had secured me a job at a very good company offering life-changing wages. I was basically hired and had already spent the money in my mind, until they ran my background check. The job I thought I had was never offered to me. Talk about disappoint?! I felt like I was invited to my own party and no one showed up. I blamed God for it all. I mean I went to church and had a hard time praising Him.

I was having a temper tantrum because God did not allow me to follow my own plans. However, that job was not in God's plan for me. Although I thought that this job opportunity would solve all of my financial needs, I could not see the bigger picture. I believe that if I had gotten that job, I would have pushed God to the side and totally depended on myself, forsaking Him and cleaving to money. I have learned that when God does not allow one door to open, that door was not for you at that time anyway. He always has something better for you right down the hallway, but we must first be PATIENT and WALK down the hallway and allow Him to open the door.

I became a youth leader at my church and weeks later received my pardon! It seemed like all of the things that held me down during my past 10 years were broken off before I turned thirty.

Romans 8:28 says *"and we know that all things work together for good to them that love God, to them who are called according to his purpose."* In 2012, I received a job offer from a very good company that was grounded in faith and serving the community. Two months later, I was promoted to a better position making better money and working in a program exactly like the one I desired to open in the future -- a residential program for homeless women who are pregnant or have children.

On May 20, 2012, I graduated from Delaware State University with my BSW in social work with my children and family watching. I have SAT and PLAYED in the fire and God has allowed me to come out not smelling like a hint of smoke and without a burn. The enemy wants us to feel like we are damaged goods; like we can do it all by ourselves and God is not there. Well I'm here to say that the devil is a liar and as 1 John 4:4 says *"Ye are of God, little children, and have overcome them: because greater is he that is in you, than he that is in the world."*

Some names have been changed

Natasha Simms

is originally from Bronx New York. She moved to Delaware in 1990 with her mother and twin sister, and gave her life to the Lord Oct. 2008. She is currently a youth-leader at Powerhouse Ministries, located in Smyrna, DE. Receiving her Bachelor's Degree in Social Work on May 2012, Natasha is currently employed by Catholic Charities at their residential program for pregnant women called Bayard House. Natasha is working on an upcoming book project called "*Just Shorts*" and aspires to follow God's plan for her life and open up an organization dedicated to helping single mothers and individuals recently released from prison.

Natasha also does standup comedy, and has hosted various events. She goes by the stage name "Tash P".

Natasha currently resides in Dover with her 4 beautiful children, Malachi 11, Shaygna 10, Shaun 8, and Nathaniel 3. To contact Natasha Simms, email her at npsimms@yahoo.com or call (410)699-0596.

Natasha's Acknowledgments:

First and foremost I would like to thank God. He has been the Father I never had; the friend who never judged; the counselor who always listened and the one love who never stopped loving me. If it wasn't for His grace and mercy, I most definitely would not be here. I thank God for the divine meeting with Kishma that brought me to this point and the many more to come. I owe my life to Him and will give Him the glory every day of it.

Malachi, Shaygna, Shaun and Nathaniel: I do everything I do for the four of you, and dedicate this to you. You have watched Mommy come out from the darkness into God's glorious light. I am so honored that He chose me to be a mother to you. I promise to push and support all of you and show you an extension of God's love every day of your lives. To my mother Debra Simms: I am so lucky to have you as a mother. You have been my biggest support and have never once left my side. You are the kindest, sweetest, beautiful person I know, inside and out, and truly thank God for your life. To my Bishop and Pastor Dwayne and Sybil Bull: I thank God for placing me in your ministries and allowing the both of you to pour into my life, naturally and spiritually, from the first day I met you. Lynette my twin, Malcolm, Sharon, Ashley, Donna, Lenesia, Ms. Ann, and Uncle Mike: You are my biggest and best support system. You're always there with an encouraging word, a correcting word and always there to remind me about the Word spoken over my life when I tend to forget. I love all of you dearly. Lastly, I thank Kishma George for being an obedient servant and woman of God and for giving me the opportunity to be a part of this awesome book that God put into her spirit. You are truly an inspiration to me and many other young, as well as older women. I pray you receive all and even more of the blessings God has in store for you. Thank you!

When New Life Begins; Pushing Past the Old and Embracing the New

The Dawning of a New Dad

Rodney Davis

Clouds thick in the sky, rain heavy upon the windshield. Wipers swish and swoosh. Horns blow. Sirens wail. Delaware Memorial Bridge looms on the horizon. Winds push against the car.

I dreaded the evening as I was getting ready to tell her the incredulous story. Even after five years of marriage, she was never going to believe me. The weather conditions seemed to line up with the words that were shortly to come from my mouth. I positioned the passenger seat of the car straight up from its usual relaxed position, put my hands nervously on my knees, took a deep breath, and tried to swallow, but couldn't.

That's when the storm started to get the best of me and distorted my vision. The raindrops on the windshield seemed to form smiley faces as if they were laughing at me. The wipers seemed to be shaking their blades at me in disgust as to say, "Shame on you!" Even the gospel-songs playing on the radio seemed to be poking fun at me. I turned on the radio just in time to hear Kierra Sheard singing to my wife, *"You Don't Know."* Next, Paul S. Morton started singing to the weather, *"Let It Rain."* Even TD Jakes' song ministered suicide to me, *"Take My Life."* I had come to the conclusion that I was being attacked on every side and even the elements and my car had it out for me.

Do you think that, I should have been able to regain my composure and look at the bright side of things? Understand that it was only by the grace of GOD that after so many years I even learned I had this daughter? Appreciate that she had been successfully cared for in my ignorant absence for eleven years? Shouldn't it have been easy to turn my sudden sorrow into dancing again? After all, I am a Christian, and an Elder in God's Kingdom. I knew that all things would still work together for the good of them that Love the Lord. But I couldn't get my mind off of the smiley face raindrops laughing at me like little hyenas, and the wiper blades shaking their heads like they were better than me.

Rain storms have a way of making things difficult to manage. It's true: when it rains, it pours. Bills add up, family acts crazy, friends turn against you. And roads. Oh my goodness, the roads. Deadly crossroads, byroads, always having to take the high roads, guilty low roads, feeling bad about inroads, railroads, dirt roads, frustrating roadblocks, difficult roadmaps, roadwork, road rage, dead-end roads, and even back-stabbing roadies. And what of those roads less travelled? Those roads of stepping up to responsibility and accountability no matter how hard the circumstance, owning up to adulterous affairs and failed commitments, admitting to a lack of integrity in money matters, acknowledging that you are still addicted to alcohol and drugs like power, sex, and money…who can praise God on these kinds of roads?

Most of us assume we can't…but is it really that we can't or we just won't? God's Word says that we can; that we can do all things through Christ who strengthens us. (Phillipians 4:13) It also says that we should put on a *"…garment of praise for the spirit of heaviness"* (Isaiah 61:3). You want me to praise You and I'm feeling heavy right now? Maybe I could praise You if I had to tell her I were getting a promotion. Moving into a dream home is praiseworthy. An all-expense paid vacation…a new Mercedes-Benz…being financially blessed, doing what I love to do -- these would cause praise to flow easily upon my lips. But praise you "in heaviness"?

In heaviness includes the most difficult times. A heavy discussion on the possibility of divorce, a heavy heart like the one you have when a loved one dies, and a heavy burden of responsibility like owning up about having another child. That final one dried up the moisture from my skin and lips. Approaching the bridge, I came out with those unforgettable words. "I've just learned that I have an 11 year old child." There…it was out in the open. Those words were no longer hanging over my head. I did it. I took the high road. That wasn't so bad. My fears were conquered! For a moment anyway.

No sooner was my spirit patting my flesh on the back for a job well done, than that I began to feel the car lose complete control over the bridge, swerving to the right. We were headed off the side of the bridge. I thought it was over. My life flashed before my eyes. I yelled, "What are you doing?" I hollered out her name in an attempt to refocus her. Usually, given out of control situations, I yell out the name above all names - Jesus, but for some reason, it didn't come out first. Actually, I think it came out in a fast second. My confession was appropriate. My confession was essential. But her response unnerved me.

At this point, we both were muddled and disoriented over this predicament. After barely making it over the bridge, my wife pulled over so I could take the wheel and drive us safely home. Pickled by the present circumstances, I missed exit after exit on a drive that was supposed to be a straight run home. The more I drove, the more I felt like I was the star in a Hollywood film. Passing city after city, I kept thinking *this mess only happens in the movies.* We stopped at a gas station and I thought *Tyler Perry could really do something with this predicament.* We left the gas station. I wondered how I could get in touch with Maurie Povich because there is no way this situation is real. Because of the silence, I turned the radio back on to hear William Murphy singing that song.

> *"I vow to praise you in the good and the bad.*
> *I'll praise you whether happy or sad. I'll praise*
> *you in all that I go through because praise is*
> *what I do. I owe it all to you."*

What a song! In the moment of my deepest despair, those words rang loud inside of me. They pierced me like a two-edged sword. If David could bless You in all times with what he had to deal with, surely, I could stop feeling sorry for myself and say thank you. Instead of continuing with my pity-party, I began to realize that this wasn't a curse but a blessing. God wanted me to find out now. She must need me. I needed her. God orchestrated this set time. God sees what's happening. God is with me. God is in control. With renewed courage, I started to thank and praise God for allowing me to find out.

All of a sudden my imagination took over: with shameful eyes, I saw my ministry crumble and my testimony unreliable. Respect as a man of God deteriorating. Reputation changing for the worse. Everyone who was for me, now being against me. My wife leaving me. My job firing me. With shameful eyes, I saw myself lower than what my enemies thought of me. In my own eyes I was as a grasshopper. Hearing whispers, I thought everyone was talking bad about me. I had become the main theme in the gossiper's mouth. The central topic of church discussions. Fuel for the preacher in the pulpit. New material for the stand-up comedian. A big laugh in the barbershop. The recurring conversation in the beauty shop. Hearing whispers, I was the talk of the town.

Feeling extremely emotional, I became bitter, dispirited, and disillusioned. Felt like running away from all of it. Lying to get out of it. Blaming to feel better about it. I felt cornered; at wits end; nowhere to turn. No one would understand. Nothing mattered anymore. Feeling extremely emotional, I felt all alone.

My imagination was running full tilt now: with shameful eyes, I see nakedness. Unbridled lust. A love affair. Pregnancy. The plot. A man's demise. A child being conceived in sin. The death of the child. Night-long laments from a father for his child. Shrill cries. Judgment. Hurt. Pain. With shameful eyes, whispering words, and feeling extremely emotional, I see, hear and feel something else. *"I have sinned against the Lord"* (2 Samuel 12:13a).

No blame-shifting. No denial. No excuses. No double-talk. I heard a confession of sin. An admission of guilt. One man being honest with himself and his sin. Repentance. I saw a man after God's own heart. The apple of His eye. I felt forgiveness.

This new enlightenment caused the storm to seem but a faint drizzle in my eyes. I remembered how the disciples went through a similarly severe storm. Replace the blue Ford Expedition with a large fishing boat, the Delaware Memorial Bridge for a Galilean Sea, heavy rains for heavy winds, and you have the same scenario. In Mark 6:43-51 (NLT) the Word reads, *"He saw they were in serious trouble, rowing hard and struggling against the wind and waves. About three o'clock in the morning Jesus came toward them, walking on the water. He intended to go past them..."*

The Sea of Galilee lies 680 feet below sea level. It is surrounded by hills that could reach up to 2000 feet where the air is extremely dry and cool. However, around the sea, the climate is warm and moist. This major difference in temperature causes the pressure and temperatures to change suddenly. Strong winds spiraling to the sea are the effect of this change. These heavy winds produce raging waves and because of the Sea of Galilee being small, the result is a furious storm without warning, and that could last up to three days.

The skilled disciples knew they were in serious trouble. What should have been smooth sailing turned into rocky road. They became like a ship tossed and driven and without a sail. Clear vision disappeared like smoke. The winds performed a coup d'etat, which is a sudden change or takeover on the sailors. They were where they were supposed to be, but were violently overthrown when the winds and the waves whipped the unsuspecting boat senseless. Quite like the prologue of my Hollywood story masterpiece. Conceivably, you are right at the place I just described? Perchance, if I said,

- Bills pulled a coup d'etat on your finances.
- Divorce pulled a coup d'etat on your marriage and family.
- The pink slip pulled a coup d'etat on your luxurious lifestyle.
- The recession pulled a coup d'etat on your business.
- Gas prices pulled a coup d' etat on your country road trip.

- Disease pulled a coup d'etat on your 5-star menu.

Panic stricken, the disciples toiled against the storm for a long time. Determined to get to the other side, they pressed their way but the storm was much too powerful. What they didn't know was that Jesus had seen them straining from afar. Perhaps, we too, don't understand this truth.

When we cannot see Jesus, Jesus can still see us! More amazing than Jesus seeing them struggling in the middle of the sea, was the miracle of Jesus coming to the disciples walking on the water. *When we cannot get to Jesus, Jesus can still get to us!*

They couldn't believe their eyes. Literally! "A ghost!" They cried. Who would have been looking for Jesus to be moon-walking on the water? Not me! The disciples didn't either. This dimension of knowing Jesus had not been experienced yet. We anticipate God to come to us as He has in times past. We anticipate His arrival in praise and worship times during Sunday services or prayer times during shut-ins. We look for God in our revivals, miracle crusades, and Power-of-God conferences. However, do we look for Him in death, divorce, disease, and depression?

If God is the God of the elements, then surely He is the God over the storms of life. His strength is made perfect in weakness or clearly seen in our weaknesses. Oftentimes, God will allow challenging situations to arise, so that He can reveal Himself to us in a greater dimension. Not only that, but effortful moments humble and remind us of our total dependence on God. In a sense, when Jesus was walking on the water, He was letting the disciples know that He was in control over the storm that had them out of control. God is in control. That's what He wants us to know. He's in the storms. He's jaywalking on the water of the crisis. God is sleepwalking on the water of the setbacks. He is cross-walking on the water of your sickness. God is the nightwalker when life becomes dismal, dark, and depressing. To God, our problems are nothing more than a cakewalk.

Thirty-two stories high to the naked eye. Eighty-four courtrooms all were being used. Human Service's finest are at work. City and state agencies sharing space: agencies such as the Department of Correction, Juvenile Justice, and Probation, the State Office of Children and Family Services.

I found myself quietly terrified at the entrance of the building. With great expectation, I was waiting to meet my daughter for the first time. Her mother had to appear in court for some reason I would later find out. Hence, we made arrangements to meet at the court. On that terribly cold day, I waited and waited. So many people walked in and out of the door that day.

That's when I looked at the clock and found out that I had been waiting for more than an hour. No calls. No text. No daughter. Just a complete waste of time.

I became a wreck. I walked around the court, going floor to floor, with no clue of what I was looking for or where I was going. I even got lost on one floor. Every step I took, I pouted.

With each new floor, I became increasingly upset. Yet, I kept looking for some clue. Some piece of evidence. Some proof that this wasn't all in vain. Then I saw it on the third floor. It was my daughter's mother's name typed on white paper hanging from the wall.

I stopped and stared at the paper. She was due in court for a custody battle that had nothing to do with my daughter, but three other children. The father of the three children was seeking custody of them. My mouth dropped. I walked over to the phone booth to call and share with my wife the new information I had learned. As I was entering the booth, I heard someone call out the father's name from the paper. Hurriedly, I ran out of the booth to meet this man. Perhaps he could tell me something about my daughter, I wondered. Before I could explain to the man who I was, he looked at me and said, "I know who you are. You're Nu Nu's father."

Can you imagine how I felt? It's much like the feeling you get when someone calls your name and has a conversation with you, but you didn't know them from a can of paint. This father whom I never met prior to now told me that I looked like a daughter whom I had never met. The next words from his mouth sent chills up my spine.

He told me that my daughter was in foster care and that she has been there a long time. I would later discover that her current placement would be her fifth foster home. And to further complicate matters for me, these fifth set of foster parents were getting ready to go through a process of adopting my daughter. I left the courthouse stunned and shaken, but I collected myself and journeyed home. In the process I lost my excitement, curiosity, and my happiness.

But I never lost my hope. This brown-skinned man of God remembered something from Psalms 27:13 (KJV), *"I would have fainted, unless I had believed to see the goodness of the LORD in the land of the living."* My faith in God told me that God wouldn't allow me to know my daughter at this time, if he wasn't going to connect us together somehow. When I finally made it back to Delaware from New York, I immediately sat at the computer to research more information from what I had gathered from that father who, by the way, did get custody of his children that day.

But would my story have a happy ending? Would I somehow get custody of my daughter who was in process of being adopted? Was it too late? Should I just not interfere with the adoption and be done with this whole thing? At least I tried, right? It was out of my control, right? Would I run away from my God-given responsibility?

Looking back over my life in high school and college, I realize I made many mistakes. I gave in to peer pressure when I should have stood my ground, lied when I should have told the truth, reacted when I should have responded, held on to friendships when I should have let go, followed when I should have led. I sought revenge, played games, didn't study, stayed up too late, broke hearts, indulged in sex and lusted after flesh, loved and trusted the wrong people. However, when I became a man, I put away childish things. Instead of skirting around responsibility, I embraced it. A child would say he has no control, but a man understands that to say he has no control is to say that he's not a responsible person. I wasn't going to make the mistake of leaving my responsibility in the hands of someone God did not intend to have the responsibility.

I created this situation and so I took ownership of it. God requires every man to be accountable in every circumstance and to take responsibility for what curve balls life throws his way. That's why I love the story of David because he too created a huge situation in which he had to confess and take ownership.

Nathan said to David, "The Lord also has taken away your sin; you shall not die" (2 Samuel 12:13b). It was David and Bathsheba. But David took ownership. He held himself accountable. The responsibility was all his. He responded with a God-given solution. *"Behold, I was brought forth in iniquity, And in sin my mother conceived me. Behold, You desire truth in the innermost being, And in the hidden part You will make me know wisdom. Purify me with hyssop, and I shall be clean; Wash me, and I shall be whiter than snow. Make me to hear joy and gladness, Let the bones which You have broken rejoice. Hide Your face from my sins And blot out all my iniquities. Create in me a clean heart, O God, And renew a steadfast spirit within me. Do not cast me away from Your presence And do not take Your Holy Spirit from me. Restore to me the joy of Your salvation And sustain me with a willing spirit."*

David would have never accepted responsibility with passive people overlooking David's faults. Had Nathan not been talking in parables and come to David about a real thief, David would have had that man killed and went on with his wrongful life. I seriously doubt that David would have come to a place of repentance. Confrontations cause us to make swift and lasting decisions. For perhaps one of the greatest moments of David's life, David made a great choice. He did what no other King had done. He acknowledged, believed, confessed, and repented. God forgave David but still judged him for the seeds he had sown. Even still, God's grace towards David was sufficient. Then the story moves us to the ultimate point of the predicament: how to come back after being convicted. *"Then David arose from the earth, and washed, and anointed himself, and changed his apparel; and he came into the house of the Lord, and worshipped; then he came to his own house; and when he required, they set bread before him, and he did eat"* (2 Samuel 12:20).

What do you do when God does not give you the answer you were looking for? God did not give me what I was looking for that day at the courthouse. It was at this moment I realized that the answer I asked for was not what I needed. Prayer doesn't change things as much as it changes us until things change. He tells us to pray without ceasing, cast all of our cares on Him, and always pray because prayer strengthens us to continue. Praying about a situation gives us courage. It is one of the weapons of our warfare. Sometimes, all we need is to talk to someone about what we are facing. *Don't just heal my heart and not hear my story.*

Our God is ever listening to our prayers. It is like sweet incense in His nostrils. We are not powerless to the enemy's perils. We have a prayer-life and a prayer-language to use to combat every crisis we face. I didn't receive what I wanted from God--a quick fix, but I got what I needed--a change in me.

God is in control and I am glad. He didn't give me what I wanted, but He gave me what I needed. He gave me strength, courage, hope: just what I needed to pursue and persevere through my predicament. In doing so, God gave me a miracle and a blessing with my name on it. He gave me so much more than what I was asking.

Yet my life abruptly took a left turn: completely derailed. How could I ever get back on track? Only God knew how.

One of the strategies of the enemy is to destroy you through the manipulation of those closest to you. Your spouse. A friend. Someone that spends intimate moments with you. If he cannot get to you through those agents, he might then try to attack you through the priests, or, shall I say the pastor, or church family. The strategy of the enemy has always been the same. He is not using any new tactics.

In my case, the enemy used my marriage. My wife and I had only been married for five years when all of this drama took place. Like any new marriage, it had its laundry list of challenges. There were challenges to manage our finances.

Communication was a challenge. Affection and romance were struggles. A challenge to take two totally separate family backgrounds and create a new one equipped for our marriage. We struggled to raise three beautiful children. Finding the right church was a struggle. Not to be outdone by the challenge of our love, trust, and commitment towards each other. In all of this, if there was ever a time I needed the support and understanding of a wife, it was then. I had a daughter who needed a loving mother. She'd been in foster care almost her entire life. Her mother, strung out on drugs, in and out of jail, producing child after child with various men, had abandoned her and never given me the opportunity to be her dad. I was furious and needed support. What I got was ridicule and humiliation in every area of my life. I needed someone to be in my corner, on my side, with me for better or worse. What I got was misery, hatefulness, and finally infidelity. I had every reason to lose my mind.

Like me, your life may have been derailed for no good reason. *The enemy is at work.* You may find yourself on the run from Kings who should have been fathers to you. Every javelin thrown is a setback. Every place you run to for shelter is a detour from destiny. You're made to run from your spouse. You become estranged from your best friend. And even in the church, you become isolated, misunderstood, and alone. Feeling abandoned, you align yourself with a mob of misfits who are as desperate and dysfunctional as you have become. *The enemy is at work.* You all sit around and compete to win the "My Life Is Worst" prize and cry about how unfair life is. You feel like you were doing the right thing and suffered this harsh treatment. Then you know of those who have been dealing wrong to lots of people for a long time, yet it seems as if they have a corner on the market of blessings. They are living more blessed than you. You begin to feel highly offended: not just by your adversaries, but by God. It seems to you like God has been letting your persecutors get away with bloody murder, rewarding them with houses, cars, relationships, and happiness. You start to believe that the wealth of the just is stored up for the wicked!

Why would God allow me to be derailed anyway? Why would he allow me to feel rejection? My wife was being used by the enemy to torture me: He allowed the enemy to attack through my wife's rejection of my daughter, through her rejection of me, and her rejection of the covenant we had entered into. Of course I was never unfaithful. I had never been dishonest about the fact that there were relationships *prior* to our marriage. I was 25 when I married. I was a good father, a good husband, and through this painful process, I found out that rejection is God's way of removing you from a situation He never intended for you in the first place.

It wasn't so much that He knew how to get me back ON TRACK as it was He wanted me on a DIFFERENT track. Through this process of rejection, I found myself moving in a new direction - along a different track.

God wanted me to go a different direction. He knew I would never "change tracks" because of my commitment to His covenant, but I was not able to see that I wasn't where He wanted me to be. We must understand that sometimes God will put you in a situation you would not necessarily choose for yourself to avoid the deadly collision He can see in your future. In order for me to move, He had to derail me.

Rejection hurts for the moment, but caused me to avoid a lifetime of continuing hurt for me and my daughter. God knows the plans He has for all of us and sometimes He will cause difficulty to come into a life with and for a purpose. We have the gift of free will, but just as we guide our children, God prevents some mistakes on our behalf as well. He has the ability to change our direction, change our mind, and change our situation by allowing what I like to call purposed difficulty to weigh in on our decision-making. I believe God allowed the enemy to interfere and harden my wife's heart so that I would start moving according to His purpose for my life.

When we identify that rejection opens the door to new potentials, we can heal and move on to gain God's purpose in our lives. Rejection hurts and causes us to look backward to what we perceive we lost. There is often a whole new world of promise waiting for us when we open our eyes to it. Even an abusive marriage can look appealing when you are not the one walking away - when you are the one being rejected. It is only in retrospect that you can look and realize that God had to allow that temporary pain to move you from a chronically painful situation. He knew you were never going to leave on your own.

No sooner did I accept rejection as God's will for a change in my life, than He set me in new relationships that I would have never dreamed could turn my life around. What I tried to accomplish for nine years in an unhealthy relationship, God immediately allowed me to gain after my divorce. God says in His Word, "If any man be in Christ, he is a new creature. Old things are passed away and behold, all things are new." I gave that old situation to God, I submitted to His direction for my life, and He made my life new again. My oldest daughter, who originally was not accepted by my wife, came to live with me at the age of 12 and now attends Delaware State University. I gained a daughter, my younger children came to know their sister, and I'm teaching in a new position with a renewed mind. I have a new home, a new church, a new car, a new season and a new me.

I made many mistakes and was bound to make many more until one day I changed my thinking. Regretting what I did in the past was crippling my present realities and undermining my future because I was not where I wanted to be. I was giving my past a penthouse apartment in my mind. My mind began to understand that past mistakes did not exist anymore, except in the place I allowed it. Instantly I realized that the mistakes I had made were already included in God's master plan for my life. God's mercies are better than rollover minutes on a cell phone. They become new every day. Yes, there were days I felt like I depleted the mercies that were set aside for me to use. Yet, there was no need to worry because the next day came with new mercies.

How refreshing it is to accept this truth. Not to abuse it, but to embrace it. Ishmael's story taught me an invaluable lesson. He was Abraham and Sarah's mistake, birthed out of an impatient spirit. His name means God hears. He was the oldest child, yet not the son of promise. He was the son of bondage. His mother was a maid servant and a concubine. He was the son of rejection. Rejected by family and society. Abandoned by his father, yet saved by God. Why did God save him? Purpose. Destiny. The pit. It was the Ishmaelites who bought Joseph and brought him out of the pit of death and despair. Only God can take an Ishmael to deliver a Joseph. Only God can take a mistake and make it a ministry. Only God can take a mess and make it a message.

Perhaps you are in a pit too. The pit of failures is depressing you and making life more complicated. The pit of messy mistakes are piling up like a landfill. The pitiful regret of poor choices and decisions has caused a cavity in your life. Engage your emotions with the revelation of God's Word. God has the power to mature you in your mess and from your mistakes turn you into one of the greatest ministers on the planet.

You can overcome trials even when the odds are against you. Know that God's grace is sufficient to bleach out the toughest stains you may be facing. Seek God's daily forgiveness. Then forgive yourself of the past because God has already forgiven you. God only remembers your sins when you choose to hold on to them. Forget the former things, neither consider the things of old. Let go of the mistakes you made and what others did to you. God will make all things new. (Micah 7:19; 2 Corinthians 5:17; Isaiah 43:18)

Rodney Davis

Is the father of four children, an educator, and a minister, and holds a BA in English with a minor in Theater. Rodney is the creator of *When It Rains*, a gospel stage play, two fellowship ministries called *The Christian Coffee House* and *Kids In Action,* and his current endeavor: another stage play called *All Together Broken*. He is the president of RD F.A.M.E., Inc.: the Rodney Davis Foundation for Arts, Ministry, and Education. He has been called to minister through his musical gifts and serves as the Minister of Music at Hopewell Church of God in Hopewell, NJ. Rodney is a worshiper above all else.

The teaching contained in Rodney's work, whether in his classroom or on the stage, is applicable and easily understood by many people. It has been his goal to surpass age, and circumstantial and racial boundaries to see that he reaches God's people where they are.

Much of his work is autobiographical and Rodney believes that in sharing hardship and experience, many can grow in the Lord. His favorite verse is Jeremiah 29:11: "For *I know the plans*

I have for you," declares the LORD, "plans to prosper you and not to harm you, plans to give you hope and a future."

Most recently, Rodney was named Educator of the Year in Dover by Omega Psi Phi Fraternity. Rodney is a dynamic and energetic example of a man doing God's work in education and ministry!

To contact Elder Rodney Davis, email him at whenitrains07@yahoo.com or call at (302)465-4426.

Rodney's Acknowledgements:

I give honor to the one I worship and adore, God my Father, the Lord Jesus Christ, and the Holy Spirit.

This work is the result of going through a difficult process and coming out victorious! I am forever grateful for the inspiration, wisdom, and example of many great men and women who have taught me how to trust God with all of my heart.

First and foremost, I would like to thank the visionary of this project, Miss Kishma George, for her valuable leadership and direction. She inspired me greatly to work in this project. Her willingness to motivate me contributed tremendously to this work.

For the development and production of this book, I feel a deep sense of gratitude to: My mother and father, my children: La Shelle, Adonijah, Eden, and Micah, M.A.D., my brothers and sister, members of Hopewell Church of God, and friends, whose faithful prayers, support, and loyalty allowed me to develop the thoughts in this work. You make it a joy to fulfill God's purpose.

Also, I would like to thank the editor for editing the manuscript and giving helpful feedback and suggestions that were critical to bringing this manuscript together.

When New Life Begins; Pushing Past the Old and Embracing the New

The Second Time Around

Ayanna Lynnay

It is often after our darkest nights and most challenging times that we receive our biggest blessings and the answer to our prayers. I have found that to be the case for my life.

At the age of 23 I married the wrong man. It wasn't that he was a bad man, he just wasn't the one for me. When I got married I was not serving the Lord, nor did I go to church or even read the Bible. I say all of that because I strongly believe that, if the foundation of something is not based on the Word of God, when trials and tribulations come it will not be able to stand.

Similar to the parable found in Matthew 7:25-27 *"The rain came down, the streams rose, and the winds blew and beat against that house; yet it did not fall, because it had its foundation on the rock. But everyone who hears these words of mine and does not put them into practice is like a foolish man who built his house on sand. The rain came down, the streams rose, and the winds blew and beat against that house, and it fell with a great crash."* The storms hit this marriage and because it was built on sand instead of the Rock, which is the Word of God, it was not able to stand.

Since I was not serving the Lord I had no clue what I wanted or needed in a mate, nor did I really know what I had to offer to a man. All I knew was I was tired of the same old same. I was tired of meeting guys in the clubs, I was tired of dating drug dealers, liars and manipulators.

Isn't it funny how the very thing we don't like is the same thing that we continue to attract? No matter how many times I vowed not to be with those types of guys I would find myself with them anyway. Although I was tired of the old, I simply did not know how to get off of that hamster's wheel. New face; same spirit, New name; same spirit. The cycle continued.

My ex-husband was the first man that was totally different from what I was used to. He was nice, had a decent job, his own car, his own apartment, no girlfriend or children. We were introduced by a mutual friend and as she described him to me I began to declare, "That's my husband!" Of course I knew nothing about him other than what was told to me but I sensed he was different. And, I wanted different at any cost. Little did I know how much different eventually would cost me.

We dated for just a short time before we moved in together. There were warning signs all along letting us know this was not the right relationship for either of us. We argued and fought (not physically) constantly. Different is what I wanted and different is what I got, so different in fact that I did not understand him and he did not understand me. We were as opposite as two people could get but the one thing we shared was that we were both hurt and broken over childhood events.

My father and I were very close and had a special bond but that all went down south when he turned to drugs. Now instead of my daddy letting me know how special and beautiful I was I turned to men to get that affirmation.

The way I dealt with my hurt and disappointment from my father was by being in one broken short-term relationship after another. I never spent time with myself getting to know what made me tick. I did not realize my low self-esteem, abandonment issues, and lack of trust for men came from not having my father around. I had trouble wholeheartedly committing to any relationships because of lack of trust. I felt if the one man who loved and made me could hurt and abandon me, well, so could all these other men. What made them any different? So I developed an "I will get you or leave you before you get or leave me mindset."

It wasn't long before I found out my ex had grown up in a dysfunctional home where he was verbally, emotionally and physically abused. As a result, he had low self-esteem and also battled with insecurity, rejection and had a fear of failure.

His issues were part of the reason he was not in a relationship. He basically had shut himself down from having close relationships with people and would just shut himself up in his dark gloomy apartment smoking cigarettes and playing video games.

We were two broken people looking for love in all the wrong places. Instead of looking to the Lord and allowing the Lord to work on us, individually, we kind of just meshed together and seemed to fill the void and lack in each other. Because of my bad experiences with men, starting with my father, I did not know how to be the wife that he needed me to be. I was hurting and broken so there was no way I could help mend or bring healing to him. He could not help himself and he could not help me.

For years he and I existed together but lived separate lives. He would be upstairs while I was downstairs. We were not affectionate with each other. It had been years since we kissed, we were barely intimate, and we just seemed to be drifting farther and farther apart. Neither one of us was in love and it showed. We were like two cordial roommates and nothing more.

Four years after he and I got married, I gave my life to the Lord. The Lord began to do a great work inside of me He began to reveal to me why I was the way that I was. He began to bring healing to me. The Lord showed me the men in my past were used to wearing me down and breaking me down so that I would not be able to function properly in a relationship. The feeling of wanting to "get them" before they "got" me manifested as control.

I had to control as much as I could in my life because of my lack of control in my life. I was mean and started arguments as a means to test the person I was in a relationship with to see if they would love me and care enough to stay and fight for the relationship. Of course most of them thought I was crazy and instead of fighting for my love, they would hit the ground running.

It was only after I started to really have a relationship with the Lord and the healing began, that I started to learn how to be a wife but, unfortunately, it was too late to salvage my marriage.

Since we both were Christians, I believed we tried the best we could to make it work. We bought and read books on marriage, watched and listened to CDs and DVDs on marriage, went to marital counselors who suggested having date nights, which we did, but nothing seemed to join us together or make us appreciate each other. One time we went on a "date" out to dinner and we found ourselves playing the games on the placemats out of boredom and having nothing to talk about. Despite our best efforts, it appeared the foundation on which we originally built this marriage was too shallow and superficial to weather the relentless storms. My ex-husband hung around as long as he could but eventually things got too much for him and he walked away and never looked back.

Newly single, I had a plethora of other issues to deal with. Our break was not cordial, so when he left, he left me with a host of bills and refused to contact me or take responsibility for his half of our bills. We had started a ministry together, and now I found myself trying to carry on singly what two people started together. Not to mention, being a single woman in ministry comes with a bunch of different circumstances. *What would people say or think of me? Would they think I was a loose woman? How could I minister to others when my marriage ended in defeat? What kind of men would try to befriend me?* After twelve years of marriage, all of a sudden I felt so alone!

I battled with anger, bitterness, disappointment and hurt. I prayed for the Lord to keep my heart soft because I knew He could not use someone with a hardened heart the way He had been using me. In my mind the demise of this marriage was both our fault and we both should have taken responsibility.

To make matters worse, I lost my job four months after my ex-husband left. Depression began to drag me in further and I felt I did not have the strength to fight against it nor did I want to. No husband, no job, trying to minister to others when I just needed to be ministered to, I found myself at my darkest hour and, at times, I thought the darkness would just consume me.

Isn't it amazing how we can hope and pray for something but when it happens we get upset with *how* it happens. I knew for years the marriage was over and it was only getting worse but the way it concluded with him leaving and refusing any contact with me, and leaving me stuck with all of the bills and no job, that was NOT how I wanted or thought it would end.

One of the questions I had during this time was, *would I ever get married again?* In the course of that marriage I learned so much about the roles of a man and a woman, as well as the things about myself that would help me to be a better wife. It was my heart's desire to be happily married. I wanted to put all I had learned and experienced into practice and have that fairytale marriage that I often dreamed about.

Once my blinders came off, my relationship with the Lord began to grow; so did my dreams and imaginations. Before Christ, I felt like I was just existed and had no clue as to what my purpose in life was; but after Christ I knew I was called to assist in the transformation process in others' lives. I began to know books, plays, movies and more were locked inside of me and I wanted to be with somebody who could help me birth them out.

I often fantasized about having the type of husband I could be a teammate with. I wanted someone who could lead and guide, someone with vision for himself, our family and ministry. I wanted to be able to laugh and enjoy being married to a man who was my best-friend, soul-mate, and lover.

One of the major issues in my previous marriage was that I was so used to controlling and doing everything and my ex following me. Of course once we started walking with the Lord, I discovered that our present life-style was out of order but because it had gone on for so long it was almost impossible to change. I did not respect my ex nor did I feel like he was capable of leading our family or ministry. I knew the next time if I was ever going to get married again my husband would have to be a leader. He would have to be someone that I could trust, respect, and want to follow.

I knew I still had some areas that I needed healing in and I could only imagine the type of man who I would be patient, and loving enough to win my heart.

I remember going to a P. J. (Pajamas for Purpose) Party. We had a time of fellowship and sharing. One of the discussions had to do with what we were believing God for. I was chosen to share but as I opened my mouth only tears came out. Eventually I got myself together and said, "I am believing God to enable me to marry my best-friend." Finally, the summary of what I wanted in a husband. *I wanted a best-friend.* I wanted someone who would love me for me, whom I loved and could truly become one with.

It is said that opposites attract. I agree opposites do attract, but for me it is similarities that keep people together. I had already been with someone who was totally opposite to me and I believed if I were blessed to marry again we would have to be a lot alike. We would have to be headed in the same directions and have a similar approach to getting there; we would have to enjoy doing the same things and, of course, we would have to enjoy each other.

That night I received a word of encouragement telling me to continue in the vineyard ministering and doing what I was called to do and my Boaz would find me and that is what I did.

I became content in being single, waiting on God. I was able to do this by staying busy doing the work of ministry the Lord had called me to do. I kind of shut myself away from men because I did not want my good to be evil spoken off. I kept my hand to the plow when, all of a sudden, I got an inbox message from a man of God.

Facebook (FB) of all places. I find it kind of funny because FB was one of the vineyards that I was working in. The Lord first led me to go on there about four years ago with the desire to minister and that is what I did. I shared with everyone what the Lord shared with me. I did not worry about who "liked" or "didn't like" my statuses; I knew I was on there for a purpose and God confirmed it time and time again by the people I connected with and ministered to. So, FB was my vineyard and the "place" I met my future husband.

I tell people all the time FB and other social sites are not bad places to meet people and can actually work to your advantage. There you can see the type of people who they are connected to, you can read what they are writing to other people, you can view their pictures, and many of their family members are also on their page and connected to them so you can get a feeling of who and what you are getting involved with. Sometimes you can find out more on a social site about a person than you can if you just meet them at the store or even at work. Of course you have to still be watchful, prayerful and use discernment but I would encourage others not to write social media and even some dating sites off if you are feeling led to go that route.

This was not the first time I had gotten a message from a man on FB but this was the first one that I felt a connection with. Even though we had been FB "friends" for almost two years, once we began to inbox one another, it still took a few months for me to actually give him my phone number.

With each message, I found myself almost wondering if this was too good to be true. This man shared his vision with me and it caused everything inside of me to leap for joy. He spoke the language I was longing to hear! When I finally did give him my phone number, our first conversation lasted over 8 hours.

Daily, we spent hours on the phone getting to know one another.

Although he was speaking to my heart, my heart was not fully ready to trust but because of his love for me and the fact he believed God showed him I was his wife, he continued to love, pursue and be patient with me.

Our relationship was like a whirlwind and many people including some family members did not understand the depth of our sudden connection. To be honest, I couldn't even understand it! I think the main battle I had to overcome was believing that this was the real deal and that God had blessed me with my heart's desire in a man.

I remember praying and asking the Lord was this "it" and He spoke to me and said, "Ayanna, why is it easy for you to believe that you will reap what you sow when it comes to negative things but hard for you to believe for good things?"

I began to believe and I received the blessing the Lord sent me. We were married six months after our first conversation. Does God answer prayers? ABSOLUTELY! But, often not in the way you or I expect. I learned that even when you can't see your way out of a situation or you don't know how God is going to work out a situation; those are usually the times when He blows your mind!

New life began when I was able to let go of the old mindset that my prior mistakes disqualified me from my present and future blessings. I now realize more than ever the Lord is able to move in your life and bless you with your heart's desire when you least expect it and you feel you don't deserve it.

I believe that God's ultimate plan is to express His unfailing love through those that we marry and are in relationships with, but when our hearts are not in alignment with His plan of love, it is impossible for us to receive real love or even embrace the love that God has designed for us.

Once my heart and mindset came into alignment with His plan of love for my life and I began to desire the things of the Lord's heart and His way of doing things, I was able to start to embrace the love that God has given me through my husband.

I want to leave somebody with a few words of encouragement. We all have fallen short and have made decisions based on where we are at in life and sometimes when those consequences come, they make us feel like we messed up so badly that we have excluded ourselves from some of the blessings we would have gotten if we would have just waited.

This is why I find comfort in the story of how God still blessed Abraham and Sarah with Isaac (the child He promised He would give them) even though they had messed up and had Ishmael (something God never told them to do).

When we learn our lessons and repent for the things we have done that were not of God, the Lord forgives us and restores us. He puts us right back in line when we get right back on track.

The Lord has a way of bringing light to your life in your darkest hour. Love is just one of those lights that comes when we least expect it. I have to admit sometimes it still overwhelms me that God had this particular man for me and he came after the worst storm of my life but now I see there was a greater purpose than what I even realized. Sometimes our hearts find it easy to embrace love, but it is our minds that we allow to make us believe that love is impossible. With man it may be impossible but with God all things are possible!

We all have a purpose that is tied to our destiny and the Lord helps us to get there by placing certain desires in our hearts. These desires give us the passion to pursue His purpose for our life. Know that if the Lord has placed the desire to be married in your heart, He will fulfill that desire according to His will and in His timing.

God has someone designed to love you unconditionally. He created us to give love and to receive it. Being married or in a relationship with the wrong person can drain us mentally, emotionally, financially and even spiritually but I am a living witness that God can send someone that will be passionate enough and love you enough to walk you through the rest of your healing and rebuilding process.

I believe that is the kind of love that God desires all of us to experience. Even if it doesn't happen the first time, thank God for the second time around!

Before this book went to print, I found out some exciting news: I am pregnant! I was married for over twelve years to my ex-husband and I was unable to get pregnant. Now, just after two months of marriage, my husband and I were able to conceive. This baby will forever symbolize new life and new beginnings to us.

Ayanna Lynnay's

zest and zeal for the Lord is apparent in everything she does and to everyone who has been graced with her presence. After surrendering her life to Christ and being transformed into the woman she never thought she could be, she has dedicated her life to assisting others in their transformation process.

Ayanna is founder The Transformation Station an online ministry & mentoring experience. She is also the founder of IGNITION the Youth Movement where the lives of many youth are being transformed as they are learning what it takes to have a true intimate relationship with the Lord and in November 2010 she launched ChosenButterfly Publishing ~ Where Books that Transforms Lives are Written and Published.

Ayanna is the author of *Devil, Please I am Not Offended {Overcoming the Spirit of Offense}*. And has Co-Authored two books *When Sisters Speak; Life Lessons from Women in Ministry*, and *Dear Lord, I Think I Married the Wrong Person-Her Story*.

Ayanna is a mother (natural, spiritual, and foster), ordained minister, mentor, author, book publisher, and so much more. She is married to Lawrence J. Moore Jr. Pastor and founder of Empowerment LifeChanging Worship Center.. Despite the many titles and hats she wears, Ayanna is most thankful for the title of Anointed servant of the Most High God.

She can be contacted online:
www.cb-publishing.com
www.the-tstation.com
Ayanna@the-tstation.com

Ayanna's Acknowledgements:

I cannot thank the Lord enough for all that He has done in my life. My life really began when I accepted the Lord Jesus not just as my Savior but my Lord. I am eternally indebt to Him. I am grateful for the wonderful family the Lord has blessed me with including my adult daughter Shakiya (wow my children will be almost 19 years apart!) My grandfather who is in his 90's and still cracking the family up, My mother Margaret, my sisters Sonya & Melody, my beautiful nieces Raven, Tayla, Micah, Kylah, my nephew Aiden, & the Moore family. God has blessed me with the best spiritual family ever too many to name but I am so grateful for Pastor Shawn & Pastor Rebecca Cooper who was there through my roughest times, Pastor Larry and Evangelist Joanna Birchett, Apostle Earl and Pastor Maria Palmer, my godsister Iyana, Mark and Danene Baskin, The Transformation Station & Ignition the Youth Movement, and my wonderful Facebook Family. Thank You KISH Home Inc. for trusting ChosenButterfly Publishing with the vision for this book Thank you!! To all my co-authors who did a wonderful job. I was blessed by reading all of your stories! Last but not least to my bestfriend, husband, teammate & Partner for life L, thank you for being persistent and patient. Thank you for loving me the way you do. There is no one else I would want to go through good and hard times with. *Where would I be without you? You make my world go round.* Love you babe.

When It All Has To Fall Apart In Order To Fall Together

April Holmes

As a young girl, I witnessed things that I would say had a negative effect on me. Being a young girl I didn't know witnessing physical abuse or the death of a loved one would have a major impact. I didn't know that walking in the footsteps of those who were placed in my life could become so easy and blinding to the fact that you don't even realize it: Shoes that were never designed for me to walk in in the first place. I often wondered how at one time in my life I said I would never allow myself to be abused and really mean it, but then, the "not me" turns into "why me". Being introduced to the false pretense of love caused me to spend years of looking for love in all the wrong places such as relationships and alcohol. The temporary fixes to numb the pain.

My parents married young. By sixteen they had already said their "I do's" before I was born. Princess is what my father called me. I was given the name, April Victoria: April means changeable and open. Victoria means victorious, victory and conquers. My middle name would play a major part in my life as I got older.

I was a daddy's girl, his only girl. I could do no wrong and no harm could be done to me. It was my two brothers' job to protect their baby sister. And if they didn't, there would be consequences. *It was that same protection I would later reject.*

I'm the daughter of a man who had to deal with a lot of his own demons and because of that it caused a lot of hurt and pain to all those involved. The memories of my parents' marriage, looking through the eyes of a little girl were not always good. There was one specific time that for whatever reason was etched in my mind. There are some things that God has swiped clear away but there are those that still remain. I call them good reminders that seem to help us down the road. This day that I am talking about was my fifth birthday. I had a birthday party. However, I don't remember my father being there for the entire party, but I do remember he showed up at the end. We were about to get ready for bed and my parents began to argue. It became louder and louder, then a knife became involved. I began to cry, even though I didn't have a good understanding of what was all going on, or what was about to happen.

It was the first time I can say I had seen the strength of my mother. She managed to get the knife out of my father's hand and snapped it in half. The next thing I know, my mother ran out of the apartment. After being left in there with my father, I had to run to go get help for him because he took some pills and ended up collapsing.

Although I had no fear of my father, at that very stage a seed was being planted, and along the way, it would continue to be watered. At that tender age things on the inside of a little girl were starting to fall apart.

There would be many more occasions that I would witness before my mother finally decided she had to leave. Being awakened at night from the loud voices and mostly cries from my mother began to really frighten me. I remember the knock on the door that saved our lives. After an evening out, we had returned back home and my father had got agitated with my mother and began to argue. She continued to get us ready for bed, and as we laid down my father told us to have a good night's sleep and told us it would be our last. He then went into the kitchen, turned on all the burners and opened the oven door, in hopes that we would not wake up in the morning.

A knock on the door came just on time. The attempt the enemy tried to kill that which God allowed to live did not work. There came a day my mom told my father we were going to go visit her mother in New Jersey for about a week, but he didn't want her to go. I believe he knew she wouldn't come back but she tried to assure him we would be back.

My mother never returned back to the Bronx. Although my mother's chapter was closed with my father, as his children, however, we would continue to have visits. My mother's decision to leave the Bronx came with adjusting to the new move to Jersey. It was good but not easy. It was good because I was now surrounded by nothing but love and a sense of peace.

It allowed me to see the better side of life that I could keep a vision of alongside the picture that was already in the frame.

Our move took us miles away where the person that meant everything to me would be waiting for us to arrive, which was my grandma, my mother's mother. She was my angel for the twelve years that I got to share with her. She was a woman with a vision. She owned her own camp, built from the ground up. My grandmother set the example that all things were possible if you just believed. *But would this example that she left behind carry on or would it just eventually die?* As for me, I was just a little girl living in a whole new world - so different from the environment that I was use to in the Bronx.

My grandma right away got me involved in the things most little girls my age desired. She was instilling in me to believe in myself that I could be and do anything that I set out to do. She wanted the best of everything for me all the way down to the shoes I wore. *I wasn't too happy about that because they were corrective shoes, as they called them.*

I always loved to dance, so my grandmother signed me and my cousin, who was six months older than me, up for tap, ballet and gymnastics. I can still hear the instructor's voice in my head as she led us into our steps. We would have recitals on big stages in front of huge crowds of people. It was so exciting the changing of customs, so many bright lights, cameras flashing and loud applauses.

At the camp she owned, I would enter into the talent shows. I always remember wanting to have the microphone in my hand and no matter who was in the crowd, there was always a big applause at the end. It all came to an end too soon. I did not know that that my last recital would actually be my last.

There came a time when my grandma had become sick, from what I was told. I remember a lot of doctor visits and few stays in the hospital going up and seeing her a few times. I used to wonder what was wrong. Why wasn't my grandma seeming to get better quickly and then they decided to tell us. My grandma had breast cancer and it would require her to have one of her breasts removed. I was too young to really understand. All I do know was I did not want my grandma to die. I just wanted my grandma to get better. Over time she did get better but not for long.

It was December 1979. There was a visit I will never forget. We were visiting back in New York for the Christmas break. But back at home in Jersey my grandma wasn't doing too well. I remember wanting to stay because my grandma was in the hospital, but mom told me she would be okay and I would see her when I got back. It was a few days before Christmas and everything seemed to be going well. Then the phone rang. A call I will never forget. It was my mother calling. She was talking to my father's mother and had asked to speak to my brothers and myself. So I just figured she was just checking on us but, no, it was a call about my grandma.

"Hi mom!" I said with excitement.

"Hi April. What you doing?" Mom asked.

"Nothing, I can't wait to come back home tomorrow."

"I have something to tell you. Grandma passed away today."

Once my father got the news, his response was not like ours. It was as if the news of my grandma's death became a celebration. So let's just say this is definitely not the place I wanted to be to receive the worse news of my life. There were some things that took place after that call that caused the fear that was starting to be familiar to rise inside of me. My brothers were not happy with our father's response, which caused them to argue and things became very physical between them. I remember backing up toward the door. It was my first time calling on the God I saw my grandma praying on her knees early every morning to so many times before.

"If you get me out of here alive, I'm never coming back." I prayed. That would be my last visit from my father as a young girl. I left angry. I left mad. I left hurt. At that time I was a little girl hating her father for what seemed to be him not even caring and reflecting back on all the bad things that took place while living there.

I know hate is a strong word and I don't entertain it at all but it was an emotion that at that age had got inside of me. I was once a daddy's princess but this princess didn't feel the same way towards her father anymore.

A girl's first knowledge of what a man should be, how he should love and protect should come from her father, but when there is a void from that it leaves a girl open to search for a father's love, all in the wrong places. That last visit put so much fear in me it would cause me to miss out on so many years of seeing my family from the Bronx and the one grandmother that was still alive, I was too scared to go visit.

At times I would begin to miss my father because no matter what I saw, I always remembered my father protected me.

The promise that I made to myself to not to ever allow a boy or man to put their hands on me was a promise I didn't keep because of what I saw. I had entered the phase of what they call puppy love but what happens when the puppy starts to bite? I was thirteen years old when I began to like this one guy. Things didn't start off bad because they never do. As the relationship continued, in spite of the warning signs, or the voices that would be in my head, this thing had to run its course until the end.

The first hit came with an instant apology. And instead of allowing it to be the last, I chose to believe the promise that it would not happen again. I never told anyone. I knew it was wrong deep down inside but I allowed my feelings for him to win. I realized later on that when you forgive, it is actually giving them permission to do it again, at any given time. I remember my lip being busted and telling my mom that I got elbowed at a party when a fight broke out. Then it was the ball that hit me when my nose was swollen. The sad part was she believed me.

Although I chose to lie that time, there came a time I wouldn't be able to lie anymore. I remember being punched in my ribs so hard that it hurt to breathe. There was a pattern now being set. There would be no bruises to see on the outside but on the inside was a different story. I mentioned earlier that there came a time I rejected my brothers' protection and during this relationship is when I did. Why couldn't I snap out of this? Why couldn't I wake up? Why couldn't all the cries of those who wanted the best for me be overheard by the force that was trying to take me on a long journey down a dead end?

In my situation I had allowed fear to grip me so hard that if I even wanted to walk away, I thought it would be the end of my life. I had to deal with being stalked outside my home, at friend's houses, at school and for those who would try to help putting them in the line of fire.

I was told numerous times how I would die and how my mother wouldn't even find my body. I believed every word of it, because a few times I was driven pass the dump and shown where my body would waste away. All I could do was hope things would change and somehow get better. The last altercation happen outside my home one night.

I remember crying out loud, "Please don't hit me anymore," as he threw his blows, "if you're going to kill me, just do it."

I'm not sure if it was the words that I spoke or the angels watching over me but he stopped. In God's Word, He speaks of making a way of escape and, on that night, He made a way for me. That night I decided I finally had had enough.

Fear is a word that can paralyze you from moving forward in your life. It can cause you to never start over and it can follow you for a lifetime when you're walking without God. So often we freely give control to other people, not knowing that it can be so damaging in the end. *If you find that you have gotten to that place in a relationship know that you are in a dangerous place.* When the other person feels as though they are losing their control, things don't get better; they get worse. My life began to spiral so out of control it was as if I couldn't see the writing on the wall.

Around this time, I began to drink alcohol. It was the thing to do with the crowd that I hung with. What seemed to be for fun ended up lasting for years until I began to depend on it. It numbed the pain, *so I thought*. At the age of sixteen I became pregnant with my first child and by twelfth grade I decided to quit school. After being in the one relationship off and on for six years, I was so broken when I finally got out of it. Not knowing back then that it takes a lot of time to heal before moving on, I moved too quickly and, because of that, caused myself more years of pain.

You can't take a broken, bruised, insecure person into a new relationship and think it will fix itself. You can be showered with the finest of everything, taken to places you have never seen before. You can wake up feeling like you finally got it right and, finally, you can tuck the counterfeit picture and frame away, but I'm here to tell you, until you are totally healed, that very thing will resurface. It's only a matter of time.

I spent ten more years on a road of searching to end up almost where I started from, causing myself more pain. There were times I had to fight off those same demons that tormented my father into not wanting to live. I became so empty and broken I remember having this feeling of wanting to be rescued. I remember it like yesterday when I decided I had had enough. I could no longer pretend. Finally the cries on the inside were becoming louder than the voices that held me captive. It was time to find out who I was and why this only girl for her father's and mother's union was kept and why was I the baby that lived.

In doing that, I had to get to the root of all the darkness inside. All the masks had to be dealt with. I learned that the only thing that could allow me to strip them is God. It was my cries for help that were answered. It was one invitation to church from a close friend who had been through it all with me. That one invitation would change my life. My search was over when I allowed the hands that created me to wrap around me like no love I have ever felt. It's when you are given that chance to fully live again and look into that mirror and love that person that is staring back at you.

When I received the Lord as my Savior, I was able to embrace the new. God allowed me to strip myself in front of the mirror and begin to deal with the ugly parts that I thought made me sick. I say that because once we strip off what we used to cover up in, then we began to see that we are unique and wonderfully made. Every inch of us makes us who we are and whom God designed us to be. That was the first step, but then there are the other temporary pain relievers. All these things have to be dealt with and handled with care as the process of change is never easy. A major key to loving me truly believes that God doesn't make any mistakes. Once you find yourself at this point where the things that used to excite you no longer do, when the masks that use to make you feel pretty doesn't, and when that temporary pain killer isn't killing the pain any longer, it's at that time when all that has fallen apart will now fall together. It knows that all the broken pieces can be used by God and out of it can become a beautiful masterpiece. It was when the good seeds began to get watered that the ballerina got to dance again and also reunite with the father she always longed for. Having God in my life filled every void that was missing. His word allowed me to forgive myself and all those who I allowed to hurt me. It was the pink pages of my Bible that sounded like love letters to me from God that watered my soul. With God on my side I was able to embrace the new and with that He gave me back things that the enemy had stolen during that period of my life. One main thing that was important to me to achieve was my high school diploma; and I did. All that I was able to survive allows me to know that there is nothing impossible to overcome with God. At times, being able to embrace the new may become a challenge but as you continue to push pass the old; you will discover that that is When New Life Begins.

April Victoria Holmes

Is a woman after God's own heart. She puts no limits on the things she will do for the Glory of The Lord. Jeremiah 29:11 speaks the testimony of April's life, "For I know the plans I have for you, declare the Lord, plans to prosper you and not harm you, and plans to give you hope and a future." Throughout her journey in life and after accepting the Lord Jesus Christ as her Savior, she began to discover whom God created her to be. From all that she would experience and survive, God placed a passion on the inside of her for women of all ages and from that she was inspired with the desire to reach back for the next hand that would grab hold.

April has taken her middle name Victoria which means conquer, victorious, victory, and placed it on her ministry of *Victoria's Daughters*. April's motto is: "One word can change a life." Life can change--through inspiring, encouraging and empowering by placing a light in a dark pit, giving strength to the broken wing--so that it can be mended for the Victorious Woman to live out her full purpose and fly to her highest height! After pain, comes healing... after the healing comes passion. She has learned to embrace her past. I am she and she is I. She has turned all her yesterdays into the best days of her tomorrows.

God has also placed a gift of writing on the inside of April. She has written numerous poems and articles to inspire and is currently working on her first book. God has opened many doors of opportunities to use her as she glorifies Him through her writing. As a little girl watching her father spend hours on his typewriter, she never imagined it was then that the gift was being developed on her inside. Mostly writing from her deepest pain, it was working in her favor to bring her healing.

April is the wife of Norman Holmes of fifteen years. She is a mother of three and a mom-mom of six. She is an active member at *Mt. Zion Baptist Church* in Salem, NJ, where Rev. Awood A. Jones is the Pastor. She is a co-laborer in *Latter Rain Prayer Ministry*. April is currently a student at Jameson School of Ministry and Theology.

April will continue to allow her light to shine to give hope to others that out of the darkest pits can come marvelous masterpieces of God. It's not where you have been that matters; it's when you truly surrender and say yes to God.

April may be contacted at victoria_daughters@hotmail.com.

April's Acknowledgments:

First and foremost, I thank God for His grace and mercy towards me, and allowing the gift that He placed on the inside to be used to glorify Him. To my husband: Thank you for all your support, encouragement and always reminding me what was on the inside. To my beautiful children and sister: It was the four of you who I had to survive for. I would have not made it without you. Love you unconditionally. To my mother, who will always will be my hero. Thank you for always pushing me and never allowing me to give up. To my father: I dedicate all my writings to you. I thank God for our reconnection. I thank God for allowing you to survive because it showed me how to survive. To my brothers: Thank you for being the men I needed in my life. To my in-laws: I thank you for always loving me beyond the marriage. Thank you for all your support and encouragement. To my Pastor and First Lady: God knew what was missing in my life and He ordered my steps. I thank you both for your love, encouragement and support. To Aziza, Gwen, Bunny, and Ms. Marsha: I thank God for all you ladies. To all who have inspired me; for those who were praying for me; for those who allowed me to inspire and encourage them, I say thank you. Lastly, I would like to thank Kishma George for giving me such an awesome opportunity to be a part of this great book project. I thank God for our divine connection.

When New Life Begins; Pushing Past the Old and Embracing the New

M.A.L.I.K
(Mothers Against Losing Innocent Kids)

Iyana Davis

I remember getting a phone call one day in 2006 from a close friend, telling me that they had a vision about me losing my mind. They saw me in a mental hospital and the only thing that would prevent that from happening was if I completely surrendered myself to God. I thought to myself that it was my friend that needed to be in a mental hospital for telling me something like that. I couldn't imagine what could cause me to lose my mind.

My life was fine in my eyes. I was healthy, my children were healthy, I was working, I had a house and 2 cars; I was able to take vacations, I was partying and basically just enjoying what I thought was the good life. For me to believe I would "lose" my mind was unrealistic so I just shrugged it off. Little did I know that just a few short years later, tragedy would hit my life in such a way that I almost did lose, not just my mind, but everything else that was near and dear to me.

As a young girl I grew up with limited knowledge of God. Like so many children, I was sent to Sunday school by my parents who figured it was the right thing to do. Although I knew about God, there was no real commitment there or a real relationship...I also obtained a bit of religion because I attended Catholic school. When I think back to those years, I realize that I developed an awareness of prayer even though I was clueless of what I was doing. Years later, my grandmother sent me to Christian high school where I studied fashion and design.

As a teenager girl, my love of shoes and fashion soon turned to dreams of being a fashion designer. All that changed in the fall of 1989 when I found myself as a high school student in Christian school, pregnant with my first child. Young and looking for love in the wrong places and under peer pressure, in the spring of 1990, I gave birth to a beautiful baby girl. Not long after that I soon found myself pregnant with twin boys. Two years later I was pregnant again with another daughter. Before I knew it, I ended up pregnant 2 more times (another son then another set of twins this time a boy and girl.) I ended up with seven children whom I loved dearly but didn't take into account with each child that, eventually, I would have to raise them alone.

It's funny because I would have never thought I would have had as many children as I did but because I did not do anything to prevent it, seven children are what I had. This was my bed and I chose to lie in it but I didn't want my children to suffer or feel lack so I did what I had to do for them not to be deprived.

I had no choice but to provide my children with the best I could. That meant making a lot of sacrifices on the things I wanted for myself and was used to having so my children could have. I didn't have any public housing assistance. There was always food to eat. The utilities were always on; and foolish as it may have been, my children always had to have the name-brand clothing and sneakers. Thinking about it now, I guess I never stopped being a fashion designer. I just designed for my children instead.

I really tried to do the best I could, but I was more concerned about the material things. Not wanting my children to ever feel like they were lacking anything, I made sure they kept up with the latest name-brand and hottest fashion, which they continued to desire even after they got old enough to buy their own clothes. As I look back on raising them, I realize I put too much importance on the material things and the one thing I didn't instill in them is the importance of having a relationship with God. Maybe if I had, their focus and some of their decisions would've been different. I now know it's not about what you have; it's about what you do with what you have.

Because it was often just me and my children, my children and I have all developed a closeness; but there was a special closeness that I had with my first-born son Malik. He would always know when something was wrong with me. It didn't matter what it was that was wrong; he knew. We had a very tight bond. He was always there to help even at a very young age. He always looked after me and all his siblings. He was more like a father to them than a brother. At times we would know things before they even happened. He got that from me.

On April 26, 2009, I was awakened by a horrible dream about one of my twin boys. I went and checked on him. He was fine. I went and laid back down. I couldn't sleep, so I woke him up and began to tell him about the dream.

He was at his Grandma's house, looking out the window talking to two guys outside. They were saying something about them having to do him dirty. Then, he appeared outside and I went to the window. He was standing there arguing with the two guys, so I went to get a baseball bat to go outside and help my son. I heard gun shots and my son screamed "Mom" as loud as he possible could. I looked out of the window my son was on his knees holding his head where he had been shot. I screamed and told his grandmother to call 911...That's when I woke up. Who would have known exactly 2 months to the date, it became reality.

No parent should have to bury a child. Losing a child is the worst pain a parent could ever experience. Gut wrenching indescribable pain is what I had to endure three years ago when my son Malik was murdered. Malik was, above all, a good boy who loved football, music, and hanging out with his friends. It was his love for music that started him rapping. Malik was going into his senior year in high school and he had plans to open his own construction company. He often talked about one day building me a house. Malik was proud of who he was and who he was going to become.

That Thursday morning, Malik got up and dressed as usual but before we left the house he sat on the couch and looked at me and said, "For some reason I don't think I'm going to be around to see my 18th birthday." I asked, "Boy what are you talking about?" He just stared at me as if he was seeing something that wasn't there. At 8:30 p.m. that night was the last time I talked to my son. He said he was coming home. He wasn't going to stay at his aunt's house. He never made it.

I got the worst phone call any mother could get, on the early morning of June 26, 2009, at 2:31 a.m. The worst news I could ever imagine was about to be told to me. The officer asked, "Is this Malik's mother?" I said, "Yes." He said, "Malik has been shot. Where are you? We are going to send an officer to come pick you up." My heart stopped. At that moment, I went into disbelief and shock. I wasn't processing what was being told to me. *Why would an officer have to come pick me up if he were alive*? I recall asking was he alive and they wouldn't state over the phone. At that moment, I knew he was gone. Still holding on, wanting to believe the worst hadn't happened to my son, I began to pray for God to spare his life and let him pull through.

I gathered my strength and called my parents to tell them Malik had been shot. After what seemed like forever, finally an officer knocked on the door. Two detectives and a lady from Victims of Crime arrived to break the news to me that my son had been murdered… Details after that are very sketchy; the next thing was to break the news to his siblings. That was the worst task I faced as a mother.

News spread fast through the community. Pretty soon the phone calls started coming in. There were numerous calls, but no answers. With little help from the police department, I started investigating the case myself. Full of anger, wanting answers, and justice, I began scouting the community going door to door every day, asking the same questions, hoping someone would remember seeing something. I needed to know who committed this act of violence.

Sadly, when it is an African-American who is murdered the media makes you feel that they weren't completely innocent, that they in some way contributed to their own victimization. While sometimes that can be true, it is certainly not always the case. I believe this kind of thinking is one of the reasons many cases go unsolved; because to the officers and people reading the newspaper or watching TV, "Blacks are always killing Blacks" and are just statistics. *I wish those people could only walk just for a mile in our shoes - hmm.*

I had to put down my C.S.I. investigation skills to plan and prepare for Malik's Funeral. Making funeral arrangements without any life insurance seemed almost impossible. I did not know how I was going to bury my son. I had no one to turn to for money, except God and, despite being angry at Him for letting my son die, I prayed anyway and asked Him to make a way for me to bury my son properly.

My resources were limited I had withdrawn all my savings; it still wasn't enough. I remember the funeral director suggesting having him cremated since he had no insurance, but my son had always said he would never want to be cremated, so that was not an option. I was told the amount I needed to come up with to have the services I wanted. I remember thinking, *"Where am I going to get this money in 3 days?"* I did not know how it was going to happen but I had faith that it would.

To God be the glory! The money seemed to come out of nowhere. Till this day, I still don't know (other than God, of course) where the money came from. People from different places donated and I ended up having what I needed to properly bury my oldest son. Malik left behind a mother, father, sisters, brothers, grandparents, aunts, uncles, cousins, god-parents and a host of friends. After laying my son away properly, now was my time to grieve.

The First Year was very rough. There were many feelings of anger, guilt, fear, revenge, isolation, emptiness and numbness. The pain seemed like it was never going to go away. I was crushed and broken and had many sleepless nights. When I finally did get to sleep, I found myself waking up at the exact time of his death, 1:06 a.m., this went on for months.

The feeling of guilt was kicking in. *Was there something I did in life to deserve this? Could I have done anything to prevent this? The list went on.* I wanted revenge on whoever killed my son. I wanted them to go through what he had. It wasn't long before everything started to take a toll on me. My hair was falling out, I lost about 40 pounds. Not knowing who had done this made everyone a suspect in my eyes so I isolated myself and my children from communicating with everyone. Fear became paranoia and paranoia began to box me in. Slowly I felt I was losing my mind.

I was empty inside; an emptiness that I still cannot properly explain. Every time I spoke with someone I found myself telling the story over and over again. I dreaded all the questions. It was like his murder was the topic of discussion. I was faced with all kinds of questions and some of them I did not know quite how to answer. The question I still hate the most was *how many children do you have*? I know how many I gave birth to, so to me, that's how many I have.

After the first couple weeks, the phone calls started to fade away and so did family and friends, like death and murder was a disease that they were going to catch. Sadly, the ones I expected to be there the most were nowhere to be found. With little to no one around, I began to pour my heart out to GOD. I had to get all the frustration, pain, hurt, and negative emotions out. The emotional baggage I was carrying around was proving to be too heavy for me to carry on my own. I was having a nervous breakdown with outbreaks of crying, illusions of seeing him and hearing his voice. I could not talk to anyone because nobody understood what was going on. It was during these times that I began to feel God's love for me. Without Him I would have completely crumbled to pieces.

Things just weren't the same without Malik around the house, so I decided to pack up and move. Two months later my children and I moved out of town. The holidays were very difficult. That first holiday was Thanksgiving, which always meant family time, something Malik enjoyed. I could not bring myself to "celebrate" Thanksgiving or any other holiday, and have not been able to since.

The Second Year I was learning to deal with things. Reality started to kick in that Malik was really gone. I still felt like I was in a never - ending tunnel - all alone and depressed. I gave up on everything; nothing mattered anymore. I was no good to myself, let alone to my other children; and being 17 hours away from family did not make it any better. It was very difficult to even look at a photo of my son without breaking down.

The people around me expected me to get over it, "to move on and live my life". I thought that to be the cruelest of all. It seemed no one really talked about him anymore; almost as though he never existed. For me he stayed alive because his memories were forever with me. When it was time for birthday parties, graduations and things for the other children, I was happy for them, but at the same time sad, because Malik was missing out of things. The pain was almost unbearable.

I thought after losing my son I would get a break from pain but, sadly, it was not over. One year and one month after losing Malik, I received a call that my father unexpectedly had passed away. My father was not just my dad but he was my best friend who I talked to on the phone daily. I had just spoken to him the day before I got the call that he unexpectedly had died. More pain: more prayer. I knew my father would want me to be strong and God supernaturally gave me strength to endure this heartbreak as well.

Tragedy, pain and grief among many other emotions were relentlessly hitting my life. I did not know which way to turn or how to make it stop. I lived in constant fear of the phone ringing and hearing more bad news. I had no peace. I had minimal strength but what I did have was the knowledge of prayer and that is where I started. *God, what are you trying to tell me? I surrender! Have your way. I can't lose another child or suffer more pain, so whatever you're trying to do in my life, you have my attention now. I submit my life to you.*

The Third Year I started to learn how to let go and let God. That is where I began to get my strength from. He gave me the ability to be able to cope with things better. I began reading scriptures, little by little, until it became a regular for me. I also started reading books on the power of prayer and effective prayers and I began to use what I was learning about God and prayer in my daily life.

The feelings of loss never go away, you just learn how to cope with them. After being nearly consumed by this, I decided things had to change. I did not want my son's death to be in vain. Sadly, after watching so many of Malik's friends die in the streets, a passion began to burn in me.

After speaking with several mothers of murdered victims and listening to their pain and cries for help, *Mothers Against Losing Innocent Kids* (M.A.L.I.K.) was born. The vision for

M.A.L.I.K. is to be a non-profit organization that would raise awareness of the impact of violence. We also want to be a source of comfort and strength to those families who have suffered the loss of a murdered child. Most people do not realize the impact, emotional or financial stress families who lose loved ones undergo. The loss of a child is a lonely experience and only those who have suffered this tragedy know how it feels. I wanted to help relieve some of this stress and be a source of comfort by providing hospital and home visits to grieving families, donations for funeral expenses, and hosting memorial events and more. Long story short, I want to be a source of comfort and strength while bringing public awareness to the pain of losing a child.

I did my research on what I would need to officially start a non-profit organization and realized it would take money, not a lot, but money I did not have. My father taught me to always have a plan B; so drawing on my love of fashion designing, plan B started to come to life.

I always had a passion for shoes and all things "bling". Putting the two together, I made my first customized shoe. That first shoe became a pair of shoes, and B'Yan Shoez "*You bring it we bling it*" was created. The company was created so that the profits would go towards making my dream of establishing M.A.L.I.K. come alive. With a renewed sense of purpose, I took to FaceBook and began to market my idea. The response was overwhelming and it wasn't long before people from all over wanted me to make them customized shoes.

It has been over three years now and I can feel my son smiling on me, proud of the fact that I did not let his death take my life or mind as well. In the beginning, I would often ask myself, *"Why me? Why my son?"* But God had a bigger plan, a plan that has allowed me to be a blessing to other people in their darkest hours. Of course at the time I didn't know the Lord had blessed me with a resiliency to be able to take all of life's blows and then surface as a victor, but these last three years have shown me that and so much more.

Yes, it still hurts to wake up each morning and continue on with life without that smile and loving nature to help me through the bad times. But God does not allow certain events to happen without reason. Had it not been for the loss of my son, I would not have the relationship I have since developed with God, nor would I have the wisdom to encourage my surviving children to develop their own relationship as well.

It has been a grueling and painful road to healing but I have my three angels (my grandmother, my father and, of course, Malik) above and with the Lord's guidance I cannot fail.

I was destined to leave my stamp on this world. A new life began for me not just on the day my son was murdered, but on the day I pushed pass my former way of thinking and handling things and began to really trust God and submit my life to Him. While I wish I could take back what happened to my son, I would never want to take back the lessons learned and the growth that came. One of the most valuable lessons I learned is how important it is to draw closer to the Lord and not to allow anger or disappointment lead us away. When we draw closer to the Lord, we are able to see how He can turn our worst experiences into our greatest testimonies.

It is only through the strength of God and the power of prayer that I have turned my pain into perseverance. Thank you Jesus, I am here to stay clothed in my right mind!

In Loving Memory of
Malik Q. Tucker

June 28, 1991 – June 26, 2009

Gone but Never Forgotten.

Leek, You will always be in our hearts.

Iyana Davis

Is a wardrobe stylist, custom shoe designer, interior decorator, event planner and founder of M.A.L.I.K. (Mothers Against Losing Innocent Kids), a non-profit organization.

She is a mother of seven children: (Quashirah, Malik, Tariq, Tyana, Marquan, Devan & De'Shante). Her first-born son, Malik, is the one who her chapter in this book is dedicated to. Although she has been through much and acknowledges she still has a long road ahead, with God on her side, she will make it through.

Iyana's Acknowledgments:

I would first like to thank God. Without Him, nothing would be possible. My mother for always keeping me covered in prayer and being there for me and my children. Even when

I went astray, you never criticized me or turned your back on me. Your prayer was always that I would give my life to God and I have done that. I love you, Mom. My Beloved Father for being my Daddy and my best friend; Oh how I wish you were here today, for I have come a long way. My children for being right by my side and understanding and not giving up on me. I love y'all. Darren, you have always been there through the good and bad, no matter what. I thank you. All my siblings, I love you all dearly. There's nothing like brotherly and sisterly love. My sister Francine: For helping me keep a smile throughout the pain. My God sister, we truly have a connection from God. That's why we are God sisters you have rode this wave out with me. When others turned their backs on me, you were still there and you still are. Chop, for all your words of encouragement and support. Maliah my writing coach, Elyse, Ms. Sidney, Tina, words can't express how grateful I am for your support. Lastly, K.I.S.H. Home, Inc.: Thank you for allowing me to be a part of this project. God Bless you all.

Iyana can be reached at:
Mothersagainstlosinginnocentkids@yahoo.com
Byanshoez@yahoo.com
609-331-9803

True Paradise

Kishma George

I grew up on a beautiful island called St. Thomas, U.S. Virgin Islands which the world calls Paradise. I lived 10 minutes away from the beach with crystal blue waters. Even though the world calls it Paradise, my life was not a paradise at all.

I was raised in a Christian home with my father, mother and brother. We attended church every Sunday morning and evenings, every Wednesday night for Bible Study and every Friday night, I attended Young People's Meetings. My parents were very loving and supportive in my childhood life. I was involved in the Girls Scouts, swimming lessons, piano and clarinet lessons, Upward Bound and the list goes on. Although I was involved in so many activities, I had very low self-esteem because of the children in school teasing and picking on me.

During my years in elementary and junior high school, the children made so much fun of me, calling me negative names and saying that I was not smart. I struggled in school not being able to complete my homework or comprehend my class work without having to attend tutoring class after school. I always struggled making As and Bs. In the teachers' eyes, I was just an average child scraping through.

In spite of all my academic problems my parents were very supportive of my education. My mom would visit my teachers at school every month to find out how I was doing in their classes. One day as my mom was visiting my Science teacher, he told my mother that I was not lazy but I was very smart and I can do anything I put my mind to. My mother left believing God and knowing that no matter what the other teachers thought about me, there was hope and I would get through school and be successful in life. My parents started to speak life into me, encouraged me to be a leader and not a follower and said whatever I put my mind to do, I could accomplish it.

Even though my parents showed me love and support, I still ended up hanging around girls in high school who were a very bad influence. They dated older men who were ballers. (A baller is a man that is very extravagant and has a lot of money usually obtained illegally.) I was a teenager looking for acceptance no matter where I could find it. Although I grew up in a loving Christian home, I still was looking for love and acceptance in the wrong places.

After I graduated from High school in the Virgin Islands, I dated a man who was 13 years older than me. He was very charming and handsome. He caught my eye because his of presence. I met him at my first job, after I graduated from high school. He paid all of my bills and bought me whatever I wanted.

In my mind I thought I had arrived, it was like a dream come true. I did not grow up poor, but I felt a need for more money because I was able to get what I really wanted to buy without being on a budget and I wanted to fit in with my friends who dated older men. Several months after dating this guy, I moved to Delaware to attend my first year in college. I had concerns with our relationship being such long distance. He told me not to worry about anything because he loved me and wanted to marry me.

As the months went by my friends from the Virgin Islands would call me and tell me that they would see my boyfriend hanging out with a woman. When I heard the news, I would brush it off, because I thought my friends were just jealous, until I started to receive more phone calls about my boyfriend hanging around this woman.

One day I got so frustrated, I called him and asked about the rumors I was hearing. During the phone conversation, there was a long silence. Then he paused and said he had something to tell me, but it could not be discussed over the phone. He began saying that he really loved me and he did not ever want to lose me. He told me that he would take a trip to Delaware to talk about what was really going on.

As days went by while I waited to see my boyfriend, I was still getting phone calls about him hanging out with this woman. In my mind, I was saying it is not true. He loves me, but deep down inside I was feeling like something was not right. The month approached for my boyfriend to visit me in

Delaware. When he arrived we went out to have dinner that night. During dinner we talked about everything under the sun, but nothing pertaining to the rumors I heard about him. As we arrived back at the apartment, he sat me down and explained to me that he was seeing another woman but he did not love her and then he began to wrap his arms around me to comfort me before he said his final words. He looked into my eyes and told me that he was very sorry for the pain and hurt he caused me but there was something else he had to share. As he continued to talk, he got closer and began rubbing my shoulders and hugging me, then he began to whisper, "I'm still married." I said to myself, *"What?! I know I must be really hearing wrong."* I began to sob really loud. I was so shocked that I asked him to repeat what he said. I pushed him away from me and fell to my knees crying. That was not all. He also said softly that he was expecting a baby in a few months with another woman who was not his wife. That was all I needed to hear. I laid on the floor crying for a few hours. I laid on the floor crying out saying, "WHY DID YOU LIE TO ME? WHY DIDN'T YOU TELL ME THE TRUTH?" I felt like my whole life had collapsed. I felt so hurt, angry, disappointed, and frustrated. I did not want to live anymore. The next week he left and I did not speak to him for several months.

One day while I was attending class, I began vomiting and feeling very sick and weak. I went to the doctor that day and the doctor returned to the office and said my test results are great. Then he said there is one thing causing my sickness. The doctor told me I was pregnant. I thought to myself *The test is wrong. I can't be pregnant! This can't be happening to me.* I started to cry as I left the doctor's office. I was so afraid to tell my family, that I was pregnant. Because of my being raised in church, I was taught before you bring a child into this world you should be married. I thought that my life was over. I went into depression. I would sit on my bed every day and cry my heart out. Months went by and I began to feel very lonely. I began to talk to my boyfriend on the phone every day, even though I was not happy with his lifestyle. I continued to stay in the relationship because I was having his child.

One day while I was cooking, my doorbell rang. When I opened the door, it was by boyfriend who had flown all the way from the Virgin Islands to surprise me. He bought me a dozen red roses, clothes, jewelry and then handed me a little box with my name on it. When I opened the box it was a diamond ring!! He asked me to marry him. My response was yes, but deep down inside I knew it was not a good idea. I began to reason with myself, saying that I always dreamed of marrying and settling down and starting a family, besides I was carrying his child.

During my pregnancy, I still received phone calls from friends in the Virgins Islands telling me that my boyfriend was hanging with other women. Every time I would hear the gossip, I would have labor pains and go straight to the hospital. I visited the hospital so many times that one day a nurse came into my hospital room and asked me what was going on in my life that was stressing me out. I explained to her everything that was going on in my life with my child's father. She looked me dead in my face and said that I need to get a hold of myself and my life. She told me that I was a beautiful woman and I had to begin to know my worth. She encouraged me not to pick up the phone when certain friends called with information about my child's father. She also warned me if I delivered my baby too early, my baby would have a lot of health problems.

After that day, I never returned to the hospital until it was time to give birth to my baby. On January 31, 1997, I gave birth to a beautiful healthy baby girl. With all the drama going on in my life, I decided to take a vacation and I visited my mother in the Virgin Islands after residing in Delaware for a year and a half. My father had passed away the year before and my brother moved to CA. While visiting my mother I told her that I needed help. I was not happy at all being in the relationship I was in. I felt he didn't know my worth or loved me the way he should.

I knew deep down inside, I wanted more but I thought to myself, how do I come out of this? Who will pay my bills and take care of my child? I did not think I could take care of myself and my baby because I was not employed.

I remember asking my mother how to get out of this relationship I was stuck in. She answered and said, "Only God can help you." I thought to myself what kind of mother would give an answer like that.

When my vacation ended I went back to Delaware. Two weeks later, I received a phone call from a friend and she invited me to attend church with her in Dover, Delaware. When I arrived at the church, I felt like I belonged there. During the altar call my friend invited me to go to the altar. While I was at the altar I heard the Lord speaking to my spirit for the very first time in my life. The Lord spoke to me and said, "Come to me today; I will take care of you." I began speaking back to the Lord under my breath asking Him, "How can I really come to you today if the guy I'm dating pays all of my bills?" I continued asking the Lord, *who will take care of me and my child?* The Lord said to me that He will take care of me; come to Him today. The Lord continued to speaking to me and He said, "He would never leave me or forsake me." Before I left the altar I rededicated my life to God.

On my way home the Lord was dealing with me. I changed my radio station from secular music to the gospel station. When I arrived home that day I received a phone call from the guy I was dating and I told him that I had moved on with my life and all ties are cut. He asked me who will pay my bills and take care of me? I answered saying, "God will pay and take care of me and my daughter." He laughed and hung up the phone. I felt peace when I got off the phone.

Several months after, I rededicated my life to the Lord; I began to find myself through reading the Bible and prayer. I began to feel comfortable with myself. I began to love myself instead of looking to men to love me. I began to see what God saw in me. I learned not to wait for people to accept me but to know God accepts me.

When you begin to find yourself, you will begin to walk, talk, look, act and think differently. I want to encourage you today: *Don't give the enemy any reason to cause you to have low self-esteem or doubt. You are fearfully and wonderfully made by God. You are gifted and talented by God. You have to learn to love who God made you to be. You have to believe that there is no one like you. Draw closer to God and He will reveal to you who you are. You are special. You are beautiful / handsome. You are somebody. You are chosen by God. Do not let anyone tell you otherwise. You have to learn how to value yourself. You have to know your self-worth. God created you for such a time as this. Colossians 1:16 says all things were created by Him and for Him.*

As I continued my walk with God, this transition was hard for me because I had to totally depend on God and not on man. In that season of my life I was working at a fast food restaurant, although I had a degree in psychology. Some of my college friends would come into the restaurant and see me mopping the floors and cleaning the toilets. They laughed at me and said it is a shame because I was not motivated to do better with myself. But deep down inside I knew I would not be working in a restaurant for the rest of my life.

I kept working at the restaurant until my working hours were cut to an on-call shift. One day I cried out to God to help me because I needed help paying my rent. I had no family members in Delaware to assist me and I did not want to be homeless. As I sought the Lord in prayer, He told me to go to a particular church in Delaware of which I was not a member. They would give me the money to pay my rent. When I arrived at the church I explained to them my situation and they gave me the money for my rent. God was teaching me to listen to His voice. Although at times it seemed crazy, I was learning to "Just do it". The Lord was teaching me how to depend on Him. I continued seeking God for directions for my life.

One day I went to the grocery store and I met a young lady that graduated from the same college I attended. She told me about her new job and then asked me the question I dreaded to answer at that time of my life, "Where do you work?" I answered, "Nowhere at this time, but I'm sending out my resume' and filling out job applications." Then she asked me in what was my degree and I told her psychology. She informed me that there was an agency hiring people for a Wrap-around Therapist position. She said that this job position assists youth in the foster care system and I should apply. My reply to her was that I had no experience working with youth in the foster-care system. She looked at me with a smile and said I can do anything I put my mind to do. I felt within myself that God was ordering my steps. She gave me the contact information and I faxed them my resume' the next day.

A few days later, I received a phone call to be interviewed for that job. I was so excited! I prayed to God the night before the interview that He would give me the right words to say. The next day, I went to the job interview and was hired on the spot! God was teaching me that when situations look impossible in life, all things are possible with Him and that I should stand still and see the salvation of the Lord.

While working as a Wrap-around Therapist, I witnessed the tremendous challenges the youth who aged out of the foster care experienced while trying to find their way to a self-sufficient and stable life. A passion within me grew for the aged-out youth and their future as I experienced their frustration in handling basic skills such as opening a checking/savings account, and empathized with their frustrations of single parenthood.

Many of the youth with whom I worked left foster care at 18 years old and found themselves homeless, pregnant, lacking self-esteem, incarcerated, unemployed and without guidance. They struggled in their transition from leaving their foster homes because many were still attending high school and were not emotionally or financially stable. There was one particular story that really touched my heart. It was then I knew I wanted to make a difference in the lives of youth aging out of the foster care system.

While working as an Independent Living Mentor, I mentored a young man who aged out of the foster care system. He had just turned 18 years old and I asked the foster mother if he could stay in her home for a while until I found a place for him to live and a job. The foster mother said to me that she would not be receiving a check for him staying at her home so he would not be able to stay at her home because she could not provide his daily needs.

We left her home that day and I drove around Dover, Delaware, until 5:00 p.m. looking for shelter openings. All of the shelters were full. With tears in his eyes, he told me to drop him off at his brother's job and he will sleep outside of the restaurant that night. When I dropped him off, I told him that I would pick him up and I will make sure he got into a shelter for at least 30 days. As I drove home, I was saying to myself, *something has to be done for youth aging out of the foster-care system.* That night I tossed and turned all night laying in my bed thinking about the young man's safety.

The next day I picked him up and I went straight to the Legislature Hall. A senator was able to get the young man in a shelter that day. As a mentor it gave me 30 days to help the young man find employment and an apartment. I continued to mentor the young man until he was able to pay his bills on his own and make the right choices. He became a better young man and his story was one of success.

As I continue working with youth aging out of foster care, the Lord laid in my heart to open a transitional home for youth aging out of the foster care system in Delaware. I laughed, *God really? I'm not business-minded. I'm very shy. I don't like speaking in front of people. God you know I failed speech class twice in college. I have no money, help and resources,* and the list went on and on. I did finally start working on the vision but stopped after four months. I told God it was too hard and I cannot do it. When

God gives you a vision it is not supposed to be carried on our own strength, wisdom or own understanding. We can't do anything without God's help. God wants us to rely on Him in every area of our life.

One day as I sat on my bed I cried out to God. I was so sick and tired of my life's situations. I told God there had to be more to life than this. My life was the same routine day by day - living paycheck to paycheck, going to work, church and back home. I knew within me that God had a plan and purpose for my life but I did not know what my calling was.

Then the Lord laid in heart to pick back up the vision He had given me, to open a transitional home for young women who were aging out of the foster care system in Delaware. As I sat on the bed I surrendered to the will of the Lord. I began to stand on the Word of God, praying, and seeking Him for direction about the vision. My faith and confidence in God increased. I began saying, I can do all things through Christ who strengthens me.

I was very excited about the vision and told a friend of mine what the Lord instructed me to do and her response was very negative. She said, "Can you really open up a transitional home without money or resources?" She told me it is impossible because I was not business-minded and had no business connections. When I got off the phone, I was tired of all the negativity. I prayed to God to send positive friends in my life. Friends who would help push me into my destiny.

You have to be very careful whom you share your dreams with. Remember what happened to Joseph in the Bible? He shared his dream with his brothers and they got really angry and sold him. Not every person can comprehend who you are in God, and what plans God has for your life. Surround yourself with positive people - - people with faith, visions and dreams, people who will inspire, empower and motivate you and help push you into your destiny. You have to guard your mind against dream-killers and distance yourself from small-minded and negative people who want to pull you down. Having positive relationships and the right people around you will empower you to reach your highest potential in God.

As I continued to seek the Lord's direction for the vision, I met someone who was very knowledgeable about youth aging out of the foster care system in Delaware. I was instructed to contact one agency and when I did, other doors of opportunities opened.

In 2008 K.I.S.H. (Kingdom Investments in Single Hearts) Home, Inc. was birthed. K.I.S.H. Home, Inc. is a nonprofit organization that empowers, inspires, heals, and guides girls and women in the community, as well as those who are presently in, or have aged out of the foster care system, and are transitioning to independent living, by providing the necessary tools needed for them to become self-sufficient in all areas of their lives. *When God gives you a vision, believe that the Lord will supply the provision.* The organization was in operation for a year and the Lord laid on my heart to host a fundraiser event for the organization.

The problem was that we had to come up with $1,000 within a certain time period. Some of the committee team-members believed that it was possible to come up with the money and others did not. I went before the Lord in prayer and meditated on the word of God, "All things are possible with God." Week one approached...No Money. A week two approached... No money. A week three approached no money... I continued praying and meditating on the Word of God as week four was approaching. We needed the money by the following Saturday. Some of the team members were in doubt and saying it will never happen; it is too late.

During week four, I received a phone call and it was a first lady from a local church who saw an article in the newspaper about the organization. She asked me if I could speak about the organization at the Women's Conference. When I got off the phone I thought to myself, why anyone would want to hear anything about an organization at a Women's Conference?

The conference was held on a Saturday. When I finished speaking about the organization at the Women's Conference, a lady from the audience raised her hand and said that she wanted to say something. She walked up to the front of the platform where I was standing and stated that the Lord laid it in her heart to donate $1,000 to the organization. When the young lady handed me the money, it was cash. I began to cry with joy in front of the women in the audience and shared my testimony. God proved Himself that day that He is faithful to His Word.

I continued my journey to walk in His Best. I want to remind you that God loves you and has a purpose for your life. Through that experience, God was teaching me to trust and believe; that if He asked me to do anything pertaining to the vision and it seems impossible, I have to remember all things are possible with God. God wants to bring us to be in a place of faith. Faith is active. It is not only good to believe but you have to put action to it. In the Bible, God showed Abram a vision that he would have children as many as the stars in the sky. At that time, Abram was in old age with no children. Abram believed God. He had faith in God's promise. To have faith in God is to trust Him. Hebrews 11:1 says, "Now faith is the substance of things hoped for the evidence of things not seen." It's impossible to please God without faith. God moves by our faith.

God showed himself faithful at the earlier stages of networking for the organization. I remember attending my first networking workshop for the organization. There were so many people there exchanging business cards, socializing and greeting one another. I felt like an outsider because this environment was so new to me. As I looked around to find the nearest seat available, a woman approached me and introduced herself. She told me her name and shared information about her business. I smiled and nodded my head the whole time. Deep down inside I was praying to God, *Please put the words in my mouth so I can tell her about my organization with boldness and confidence.* When she was finished sharing details about her business, she asked me about my business. I took out my business card and a pamphlet and I started to share with her the mission and vision of the organization. While I was explaining the organization to her, she had tears streaming down her face. The woman interrupted me and said with tears in her eyes that before she attended this workshop she prayed to God for a divine connection. She said that she loved the mission and the vision. She also told me that she had money and wanted to donate the money to the right organization. We exchanged numbers and she kept her word. Months after she donated a large amount of money towards the organization. God again showed up like never before!

As I continued seeking the face of God in prayer for the direction for the organization, He laid on my heart to provide another service within the organization called *Women Destined for Greatness* that would provide empowerment and inspiration for teen girls and young women ages 13-25 in the community in Delaware.

The vision God gave me for the mentoring program is to serve as a catalyst to inspire young women to discover their self-worth, and build their self-esteem and self-confidence. God continued to order my steps and place the right people to mentor and volunteer for the mentoring programs. The first workshop the mentoring program held, only two girls showed up. I kept going and as I continued hosting the workshops,

God gave me strategic ideas of how to market the workshops and the events the organization hosted.

As time went by, the organization was recognized in different newspapers throughout Delaware for empowering girls and women. As the months went by, more girls and young women began to attend the workshops and a couple of the organization events were sold out.

I would like to encourage you today that when you have a dream you have to pursue, pursue, pursue because with God all things are possible. If God gave you a vision, do not despise small beginnings, God will put His "super" on top of your "natural".

Months went by and the Lord continued to place people in my life to assist me with the vision. One day as I was seeking God in prayer, He laid in my heart to build the transitional home from the ground up. This time when I heard the voice of the Lord, I did not question, I answered and said YES Lord! The organization did not have money to purchase land or to start building the home. I was not connected to a home contractor to help with the vision. Nor did I have any idea how to begin to network with a home-builder. What I did not realize is that God was teaching me how to walk by faith and not by sight, even the more.

God wanted me to totally trust Him. I continued praying, fasting and meditating on the Word of God. One day I received a phone call from the owner of a home-builder company in Delaware. He stated that he saw the organization in the newspapers and was drawn to help build the transitional home for the organization. While I was listening to the owner speak, tears were running down my face and I was praising God for proving Himself, that when He speaks, *it will come to pass, no matter how it looks.*

Throughout all of the pain, struggles and tribulations I endured, God showed me that there is purpose in my pain and He has a plan for our life no matter how people negatively label us or what they think about us. I came a long way from having low self-esteem, being a single mom with no hope, and not knowing how I would provide a roof over my head, to having a dream to provide housing for young women aging out of the foster care system. I am determined to see that dream fulfilled. Romans 8:28 *says all things work together for good to them that love God.* I want to encourage you today that God loves you and has a purpose and a plan for your life. Don't give up! Don't lose hope! Stand on God's Word like never before! Continue to walk and seek God no matter what your life circumstances look like or how you feel right now. Remember that you are truly destined for greatness and there is greatness inside of you.

I was born and raised in the place most people call paradise but after all I have been through, I have learned true Paradise comes when you began to push beyond your own limitations, trusting God completely and living the life He created you to live.

Kishma A. George

is the President/CEO of K.I.S.H. Home, Inc., Director of Women Destined for Greatness Mentoring Program. Ms. George was born in the U.S. Virgin Islands and currently resides in Delaware. She obtained a Bachelor of Science degree in Psychology from Delaware State University. Ms. George is presently a Senior Social Worker/Case Manager in Delaware. Her extensive background in the Human Services community includes serving in the capacity of an Independent Living Mentor and a Wrap-around Therapist. During her tenure as a mentor and Wrap-around Therapist, she noticed the limited amount of community resources offered to the transitioning youths who often became vulnerable to homelessness, poverty, incarceration, and premarital pregnancy.

Ms. George wanted to make a difference in their lives and make certain that they had a safe, successful transition to adulthood and independent living. Thus, K.I.S.H. Home, Inc. was birthed to bridge the gap between leaving the foster care system and securing a stable future for many of these young women.

Ms. George is a motivational speaker, mentor, playwright, producer and aspiring author whose mission is to inspire and encourage women and girls to fulfill their God-given purpose. Her works as a speaker and mentor are executed through the Women Destined for Greatness Mentoring Program and collaboration with the juvenile and school system in Kent County, DE. She believes that regardless of life's circumstances, there is greatness inside of every woman. Ms. George, not only the visionary, but the esteemed writer, director and producer of the inspirational stage play *When You Have A Dream* in which she starred in a leading role.

Her diligence and passion for young women has been recognized in various newspaper articles, including the Dover Post, Delaware News Journal and Milford Beacon. Ms. George was also featured in BOND, Inc. blogspot week's spotlight "*Fostered Out of Love*". Additionally, she is the recipient for the 2011 **Empowered Women of the Year Award** by Empowered Women Ministries and Woman of the Year 2011- 2012 by Zeta Phi Beta Sorority, Inc. / Theta Zeta Zeta Chapter in recognition of outstanding contributions to the Greater Dover Community.

Ms. George is the proud mother of an intelligent, God-fearing and aspiring entrepreneur daughter. Her activities outside of K.I.S.H. Home, Inc. include but are not limited to being an active member of Bread of Life Christian Church under the leadership of Bishop Ronald Richardson and Pastor

Faye Richardson where she is serving as an Evangelist. Additionally, she serves on the board of directors for Inspirations for Women, Inc. in Maryland. She has also toured with the gospel stage play, When it Rains; a Rodney Davis Production.

Kishma A. George can be reached at:
Email: kgeorge@kishhomeinc.org
Website: www.kishhomeinc.org
Mailing Address: P.O.BOX 672, Felton, DE 19943

Kishma's Acknowledgments:

First and foremost I want to give God all the glory and honor who made this vision possible. I love you Lord! In memory of my beloved father, Edmond George: I am thankful for his encouragement and inspiring me to dream. To the best mother in the world, Novita George: I thank you for your love, support, encouraging words and praying for me. Thank you for not giving up on me. I love you Mom. To my wonderful, daughter, Kiniqua, I love you dearly. Thank you for your encouraging words, hugs and love. To my family: James, Raeisha, Christopher, Joshua and Janisha, thank you for supporting the vision with your prayers and love. Thank you to my Bishop Ronald & Pastor Faye Richardson for your prayers, encouraging words and support. To Bread of Life Christian Church & the Single's Ministry: Thank you for your prayers, support and encouraging words. A special thank you to the co-authors of this book: Rodney Davis, Ayanna Lynnay,

About KISH Home Inc,

Letisha Galloway, April Holmes, Natasha Simms, & Iyana Davis. Thank you for sharing your story, dedication and believing in the vision. Thank you Toy James, Abena Mc Clean & Jamila Milbourne: Thank you for your prayers, support and encouraging me to pursue my dreams. I thank God that you all are my friends. To Trina Bowers, Shanda Ayoub and Yakini Blandford: Thank you for all your support, love, prayers and encouragement. To Joyce Dungee Proctor: Thank you for all of your support for K.I.S.H. Home, Inc.'s vision and for your encouraging words. To K.I.S.H. Home, Inc.'s Board/Advisors, Volunteers & Mentors: Thank you for your dedication, support and believing in the vision in helping make a difference in the young women lives in Delaware. To Les Brown: Thank you for all of your support for K.I.S.H. Home, Inc.'s vision and your encouraging words. To Soprona Pickering: Thank you for your tireless support, love and encouragement. Thank you so much for supporting K.I.S.H. Home, Inc.'s vision. To Christian Richardson: I thank you for your support and assistance in the vision. God bless you. To Pastor Ayanna, publisher: I thank God every day for bringing you into my life. You have been a blessing. Thank you for your encouraging words, support, love and believing in the vision. Lastly, I would like to thank CTS graphics Chante, Steve Lopez, Nashana Wiggins and to everyone that encouraged, prayed and supported K.I.S.H. Home, Inc. over the years, I am forever grateful. God bless!

When New Life Begins; Pushing Past the Old and Embracing the New

About KISH Home Inc.

Kingdom Investments in Single Hearts (K.I.S.H.) Home, Inc. was founded in August 2008, out of the desire to make an impact in the lives of girls & women in the community as well as those young women who are presently in, or have aged out of the foster care system in Delaware. Through Ms. George's works as an Independent Living Mentor, she has mentored young adults. During her tenure as a mentor, she witnessed the tremendous challenges these young people experienced while trying to find their way to a self-sufficient and stable life.

A passion within her grew for these young adults and their future, as she experienced their frustration in handling basic skills, such as opening a checking/savings account, parenting and the frustration of single parenthood. Ms. George knew that these young adults, whether they were a single parent or single, needed a strong support system that would empower and encourage them to take control of their lives. They struggled in their transition of leaving their homes or foster care because many were still attending high school and were not emotionally or financially stable.

After witnessing this, Ms. George began her journey of seeking ways to assist young adults in becoming emotionally and economically self-sufficient so that their transition out of their homes or the foster care system and into independent living was successful. Many of the young adults with whom she worked left their homes or foster care at 18 years old, and found themselves homeless, pregnant, lacking self-esteem, incarcerated, unemployed and without guidance. As a mentor, Ms. George became frustrated by the minimum amount of resources the community offered these young adults. She wanted to make a difference in their lives and make certain that they had a safe, successful transition to adulthood and independent living.

K.I.S.H. Home, Inc. offers young women in Delaware the support they need to become emotionally stable and self-sufficient in every aspect of their lives and community.

Once again K.I.S.H. Home, Inc. would like to thank you for the purchase of this book. Portions of the proceeds will be going to K.I.S.H. Home, Inc. a 501 (c) 3 non-profit, faith-based organization that is currently raising funds to purchase a 24-hour supervised residential home for young women ages 18-23 who are presently in, or have aged out of the foster care system in Delaware. If you would like to help make this transition home happen, you can send your donations to K.I.S.H. Home, Inc., P.O. BOX 672, Felton, DE 19943 or www.kishhomeinc.org

www.ingramcontent.com/pod-product-compliance
Lightning Source LLC
Chambersburg PA
CBHW071701040426
42446CB00011B/1854